ARTintegration

MULTIDISCIPLINARY LESSONS THAT TEACH ACROSS THE CURRICULUM THROUGH ART

Library of Congress Cataloging-in-Publication Data

Holland, Debbie.
 ARTintegration : multidisciplinary lessons that teach across the curriculum through art / Debbie Holland. — First [edition].
      pages cm
 Includes bibliographical references and index.
 ISBN 978-1-56290-692-4 (alk. paper)
 1. Art—Study and teaching (Elementary)—Activity programs. I. Title.

 N362.H65 2012
 372.5'044—dc23

                              2012023171

Copyright © 2012 by Crystal Productions Co.
All Rights Reserved

ISBN 978-1-56290-692-4
Printed in Hong Kong

MULTIDISCIPLINARY LESSONS THAT TEACH ACROSS THE CURRICULUM THROUGH ART

DEBBIE HOLLAND

ARTintegration

TABLE OF CONTENTS

- **FLORAL PRINTS** (Science/Social Studies) 4-5
- **TEXTILE DESIGN COLORING** (Textile Design/Science) 6-7
- **PLAIDS AND STRIPES FOREVER** (Textile Design/Math) 8-9
- **GOTHIC STYLE STAINED GLASS** (Social Studies/Math/Architecture) 10-11
- **SEURAT'S DOTS** (Art/Social Studies/Science 12-13
- **DESIGNER PLAIDS** (Art/Textile Design/Math) 14-15
- **ILLUSTRATED CAT** (Illustration/Language Arts) 16-17
- **DRAGON CREATIONS** (Illustration/Social Studies) 18-19
- **THE HUMAN BODY AND ORGANS** (Science/Social Studies) 20-21
- **MORPHED BUGS** (Science/Language Arts) 22-23
- **HIPPOGRIFF ILLUSTRATIONS** (Illustration/Language Arts) 24-25
- **MEXICAN WOVEN CLOTH** (Textile Design/Social Studies/Math) 26-27
- **ARCS AND PROTRACTORS** (Math/Social Studies) 28-29
- **CRAZY QUILTS** (Textile Design/Social Studies/Math) 30-31
- **DYNAMIC DIAMONDS** (Math/Social Studies) 32-33
- **DOTS FOREVER** (Textile Design/Math) 34-35
- **GINGERBREAD HOUSES** (Math/Language Arts/Architecture) 36-37
- **PAISLEY POWER** (Textile Design/Social Studies/Math) 38-39
- **ANGEL WRAP** (Design/Social Studies/Math) 40-41
- **PERSONAL CARTOUCHE** (Art/Social Studies/Language Arts) 42-43
- **SANTA PAINT STICKS** (Crafts/Social Studies/Language Arts) 44-45
- **PENNSYLVANIA DUTCH FOLK ART** (Art/Pottery/Social Studies) 46-47
- **THAYER: FATHER OF CAMOUFLAGE** (Art/Science/Language Arts 48-49
- **PUEBLO TALE** (Design/Social Studies/Language Arts/Math) 50-51
- **CONTEMPORARY SCULPTURES** (Art/Social Studies/Math) 52-53
- **MONDRIAN: NONOBJECTIVE ART** (Art/Math) 54-55
- **LINEAMANIACS** (Design/Math/Social Studies) 56-57
- **WALL ART** (Art/Social Studies/Science) 58-59
- **SILHOUETTE** (Social Studies/Science) 60-61
- **COLOR INTERACTION** (Art/Science) 62-63
- **NATIONAL STANDARDS FOR THE VISUAL ARTS** 66-67
- **GLOSSARY** 68-71

INTRODUCTION

Lesson planning is one of the things I love doing the most in life! When ideas and input and experience combine and morph into new ways to present curriculum, the excitement for teaching increases. Doing the same lessons every year has never been an option for me and I consider myself very lucky to have always been able to create new lessons each year. I know teachers who love teaching, but who don't always have the time or energy to come up with new ideas for their lessons. This book is for them and for others who see how art can and should be used to teach everything! For me, all subjects overlap into other curriculum areas. Teaching art like this is a holistic way of teaching elementary children and reaches students with their multiple ways of learning.

My classes are 45 minutes long. Students come into the room checking out art materials on the tables to be used in the lesson…and sit on a carpet in the front of the room. There they see art prints of the masters we are studying. We list the elements of art and underline them if they are being used in the project. They then call out the primary colors…followed by secondary colors…warm colors…cool colors…complementary colors and how to create neutral colors. I use this introduction as a way to cover art theory and show students how it relates to the day's project. I have laminated words with the names/colors that are placed on the board as students are called on to contribute. Under "Value", there is a sticker for tint and shade. This allows for many individual students to participate and only takes a few minutes. We compare/contrast artists and their work for ten minutes or less. Then I introduce the techniques or theme of the lesson, and present a key word or words for each project. In addition, I include a list of "criteria" for successful artwork for each lesson that students can use to assess themselves as they work. I present new art projects each week so students are exposed to a variety of art materials or media. All the work in this book was done in one class. When you see the word "check" in the steps, it means it is crucial to check students' work before they continue.

There are great resources out there now to use both online and off! It is my hope that these 30 lessons will be great input for you and make your teaching experience even more enjoyable. They were written to cover school, county, state, and national art concerns. Adapt them to best fit your needs…hopefully they will make your year a little easier!

Floral Prints
Science/Social Studies

criteria:
- Must use horizon/table line
- Must use printing process
- Can use any colors

ELEMENTS OF ART:
Line, Shape, Color, Value, Texture, and Space

MATERIALS:
Large black construction paper, day glow paints, paper plates, paper towels, Styrofoam pieces

REFERENCE:
Art prints, textile floral patterns (painted and printed)

VOCABULARY:
Floral, flower, composition, apprentice, palette, still life, print

ESSENTIAL QUESTIONS:
What does "floral" mean?
What does composition mean?
How are these artists' floral paintings different or the same?

NATIONAL STANDARDS: 1, 2, 3, 4, 5, 6

LEARNING OBJECTIVES:
To compare and contrast different artists' ways of painting a floral theme. To create a floral composition using a printmaking technique.

INFORMATION:
RACHEL RUYCH (1664-1750) Dutch
- raised in a home that fostered her talents as an artist
- began painting at 15 years old. Was one of the most gifted still life and floral painters in Holland. Prices were higher than Rembrandt!
- was an apprentice to a master which was rare for a woman
- best known for her meticulous methodical painting with lots of detail
- Painted while married with 10 kids and kept maiden name for her signature!

PIERRE BONNARD (1867-1947) French
- was a law student who transferred to Beaux-Arts
- part of a group called the Nabis (prophets)
- attracted by the color of the Impressionists but never forgot form & reality
- loved ordinary objects & actions
- known for his exquisite palette

ODILON REDON (1840-1916) French
- solitary artist who the Symbolist artists discovered and claimed as theirs
- master of etching & lithography
- "visual poems" evoking dark world of Edgar Allan Poe

After discussing similarities & differences of these floral still-lifes, students will create their own printed floral compositions.

Key word Floral

STEPS:
- sketch layout
- check work
- print light to dark
- wash hands

ARTintegration

student work

Textile Design Coloring
Textile Design/Science

> **Criteria:**
> - Must have color tab boxes
> - Can mix any values
> - Paint flat strokes

ELEMENTS OF ART:
Line, Shape, Color, Value, Texture, and Space

MATERIALS:
Paper towels, Q-tips, brushes, water jars (detergent scoopers), rulers, pencils, paint cups (blue, yellow, red, green, orange, purple, white, black), plastic palettes

REFERENCE:
Examples of textile design artwork and painted & printed colorings

VOCABULARY:
Textile, design, designer, coloring, primary, secondary, complementary, tint, shade, geometric, floral

ESSENTIAL QUESTIONS:
What is a coloring?
What do Textile Designers do for a living?
What is negative space?
What are the primary colors?
What are the secondary colors?
What are the warm colors?
What are the cool colors?
What are complementary colors?

NATIONAL STANDARDS: 2, 3, 5, 6

LEARNING OBJECTIVES:
To explore the color wheel by mixing tints and shades of colors.

To create a "coloring" for a floral pattern.

INFORMATION:
Textile designers are asked to be creative and come up with designs whether they were floral, stripes, textures, or geometric. Sometimes they are given pictures or samples that a customer likes and wanted me to copy the general feeling of the pattern in color and design. The pattern would have to have significant changes so there wouldn't be any copyright problems. The fun part when doing this type of work was the colorings or different color combinations that needed to be done for each pattern (usually at least 3). Look at some examples of textile design on the internet or in books.

Choose a textile design and act as designer to trying to improve the combination of colors. Use Q-tips to transfer paint from cups to your palettes. Then use your brush to mix your desired tint or shade of a color. Paint in the boxes and area in your design where you want the color to be.

*Review color wheel: Primary/secondary/complementary/tint/shade and show how to mix the colors.

Key word coloring

STEPS:
- use ruler for boxes at bottom
- use Q-tips
- mix & paint with brush
- rinse brush

ARTintegration

student work

Plaids and Stripes Forever
Textile Design/Math

criteria:
- Lines must be parallel
- Can scratch out color in plaid
- Can scratch thick or thin lines

ELEMENTS OF ART:
Line, Shape, Color, Value, Form, Texture, and Space

MATERIALS:
White Scratch-Art paper, sticks, scrap paper, pencil, eraser, glue, colored construction paper

REFERENCE:
Stripes/plaid textile artwork and swatches, wrapping paper designs

VOCABULARY:
Vertical, horizontal, parallel, intersect, perpendicular, warm, cool, primary, secondary

ESSENTIAL QUESTIONS:
What do parallel lines look like?
What are vertical lines?
What are horizontal lines?
What does it mean when lines intersect?

NATIONAL STANDARDS: 2, 3, 5, 6

LEARNING OBJECTIVES:
To identify and draw parallel/vertical & horizontal lines. To create a stripe or plaid pattern.

INFORMATION:
This week we will watch lines do some amazing things because of their placement AND because of some wonderful scratch art paper. Using lines in different arrangements, different degrees of thickness and colors, we created many stripe patterns. Let's look at some of the cloth examples. By having the lines crisscross each other (vertically & horizontally) we created beautiful plaids.

There are a variety of ways you can work today. Let's see how many possibilities we can come up with before you use the good paper. First, sketch (with ruler if desired). Then place the scrap over the good paper & trace. If you would rather use markers for one set of parallel lines, do those first.

Key Word
Parallel

STEPS:
- sketch
- check
- trace
- markers
- scratch with stick
- mount on construction paper

ARTintegration

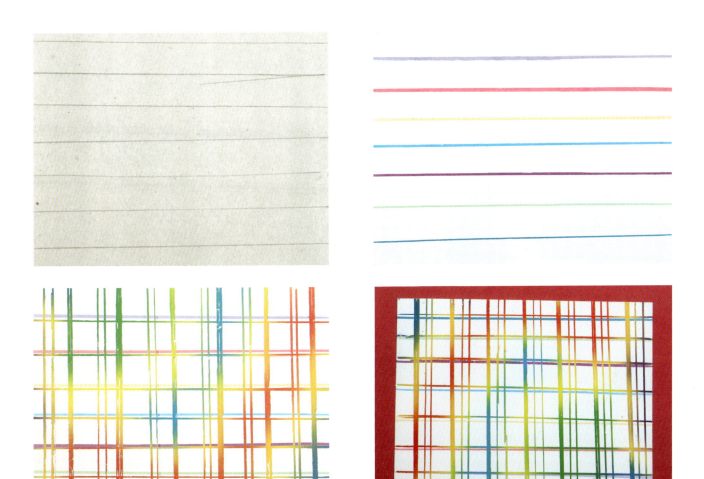

student work

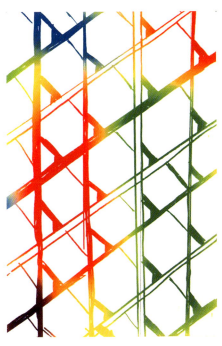

Gothic Style Stained Glass
Social Studies/Math/Architecture

> **criteria:**
> - Must use simple shapes
> - Must have Gothic arch
> - Can vary thickness of lead lines

ELEMENTS OF ART:
Line, Shape, Color, Value, Form, Texture, and Space

MATERIALS:
Stained glass scratch art paper, sticks, scrap manila paper, eraser, pencil

REFERENCE:
Laminated stained glass designs from books, Rose window from Notre Dame, any books with gothic stained glass

VOCABULARY:
Renaissance, cathedral, Romanesque, Gothic, symmetrical, architecture, arch, glass, lead, guild, bishop, gargoyles

ESSENTIAL QUESTIONS:
What is architecture? How is the Gothic style of architecture in cathedrals different from the earlier Romanesque arch? What is a guild? Why did they create gargoyles?

NATIONAL STANDARDS: 1, 2, 3, 4, 5, 6

LEARNING OBJECTIVES:
To use simple basic shapes to create symmetrical stained glass.

INFORMATION:
As the Middle Ages progressed, a major change took place in the architecture of the churches and cathedrals. During the 800-1100s, places of worship were built in the Romanesque style, with round arches, thick walls, and columns erected close together. Heavy stone walls surrounded and supported the arched passageways making the interiors dark and damp. In the latter part of the Middle Ages (1100-1400) Gothic Architecture became prominent. Pointed arches, thinner walls, and incredibly beautiful stained glass were created. The spiritual feeling produced by cathedrals such as Notre-Dame in Paris was very much in keeping with the importance placed on religion at this time.

The Romanesque style in the early Middle Ages changed people's thinking about the purpose of art. Gone were the attempts to portray the human form as a perfect physical specimen as the ancient Romans and Greeks did. Man's spiritual perfection was considered more important. Folds of robes became stiff, convoluted design elements rather than realistic draping over living forms. This thinking still affected the way later Gothic artists designed sculptures and stained glass windows for their new cathedrals. Though the windows themselves were huge to fit into the spaces between the arches, they were actually made up of many tiny pieces of colored glass cut to fit together like a jigsaw puzzle and held with strips of lead. Today we will design a simple, symmetrical stained glass design using scratch art paper.

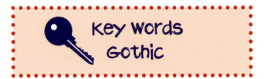

> **Key words**
> Gothic

STEPS:
- fold manila paper in half
- sketch outline and shapes (5-6 lines)
- popsicle stick — rub to transfer
- white/black — trace shapes with pencil
- stick — scratch out shapes

ARTintegration

student work

Seurat's Dots

Art/Social Studies/Science

> **Criteria:**
> - Use basic shapes for fruit
> - Fruit on or overlapping table line
> - Add highlights/shades/shadows

ELEMENTS OF ART:
Line, Shape, Color, Value, Form, Texture, and Space

MATERIALS:
Half of white construction sheet, popcorn, plates, pencil, paint (blue/yellow/red/green/orange/purple)

REFERENCE:
Georges Seurat, *A Sunday on La Grande Jatte* and studies, *The Seine at the Grande-Jatte*, *The Harbor at Honfleur*

VOCABULARY:
Pointillism, texture, primary, secondary, relief sculpture, geometric shapes, complementary, warm, cool

ESSENTIAL QUESTIONS:
Who was Georges Seurat?
What do his paintings look like?
Why would an artist choose to paint only with dots/dabs? What happens when the dots are put close together? How about far apart?

NATIONAL STANDARDS: 1, 2, 3, 4, 5, 6

LEARNING OBJECTIVES:
To create a still life of various types of fruit using basic shapes painted in Seurat's style.

INFORMATION:
GEORGES SEURAT (1859-1891), French

In the beginning we have the dot! A dot can be used for texture or can be repeated close together to make a <u>line</u> which can become an <u>outline</u> and form a <u>shape</u>. Some artists work only with dots; some work with splotches or brushstrokes. Georges Seurat worked around the time of the Impressionists who painted with visible brushstrokes. Seurat studied science and color theory and developed a style of painting with dots that required special placement of dots of color.

Today we will create pictures in a similar style of Seurat's work. Fruit compositions (using simple shapes) will be your starting point. Then we will print using popcorn dipped in different colors.

Key word Seurat

STEPS:
- sketch
- print light to dark

ALTERNATE PROJECT (Grades 3-5): Use watercolor paints and Q-tips with fruit still life composition

ALTERNATE PROJECT (3-5): Use acrylic paint with Dollar Tree brushes (cheap brushes!)

ALTERNATE PROJECT (K-2): Use bingo dots (Dollar Tree) with fruit or floral theme

ALTERNATE PROJECT (K-5): Use textured "rings" from an art suplly store or company

ARTintegration

student work

Designer Plaids
Art/Textile Design/Math

Criteria:
- Must use ruler to measure (not just line from width of ruler)
- Can have multiple lines in stripe or plaid
- Can cut colored shapes for design

ELEMENTS OF ART:
Line, Shape, Color, Value, Form, Texture, and Space

MATERIALS:
Black construction paper, ruler, white colored pencil, Lick-A-Stick shapes

REFERENCE:
Examples of fabric and printed plaids, works by Piero Dorazio

VOCABULARY:
Designer, plaid, woven, loom, warp, weft, positive space, negative space, balance, perpendicular, parallel, vertical, horizontal

ESSENTIAL QUESTIONS:
What does parallel mean?
What does perpendicular mean?
What does intersection mean?

NATIONAL STANDARDS: 1, 2, 3, 4, 5, 6

LEARNING OBJECTIVES:
To create a designer plaid with measured lines and basic shapes.

INFORMATION:
We have been talking about textures created from dots, dashes and lines for the past 3 weeks. When we talked about weaving last week, which set of lines were the warp? Which set of lines are the weft? Today we are going to create a woven look for the background space. The plaid will be measured and done in one colored pencil. (Show reference and compare/contrast.) This one cannot be folded or marked….you will have to take time to measure! Then we will create a design on top of that with the shapes of different colors. Demonstrate the process.

Key word Design

STEPS:
- measure 1-inch segments across paper with pencil and mark with dots/dash vertically
- connect dots with pencil
- repeat process horizontally (can do a different width)
- lick and apply shapes

Alternate Project (4-5): Use one-inch lines for grids. Call out coordinate points for placement of the colored shapes for upper grade classes.

ARTintegration

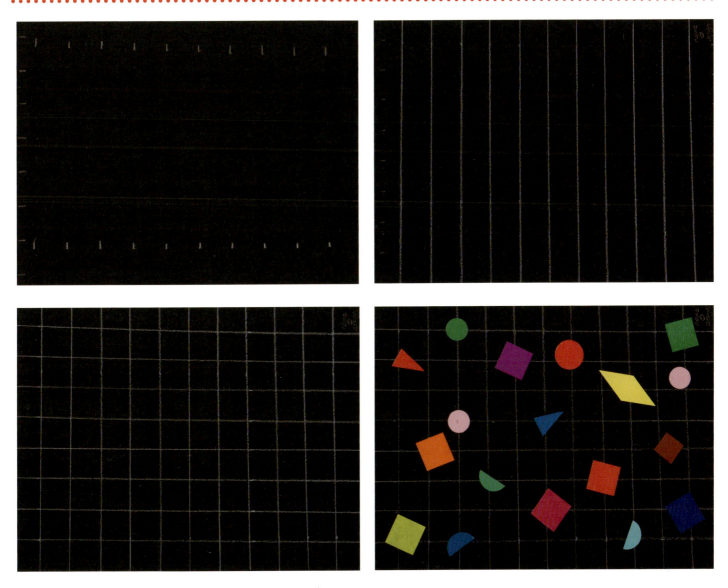

student work

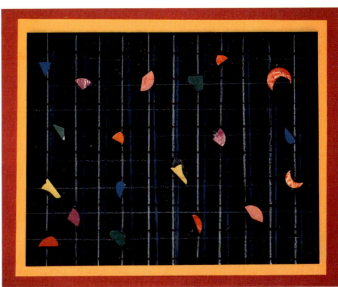

17

Illustrated Cat
Language Arts

> **Criteria:**
> - Pay attention to positive and negative space
> - Must try Y-shaped tree with sketch
> - Can choose any colors for your illustration

ELEMENTS OF ART:
Line, Shape, Color, Value, Form, Texture, and Space

MATERIALS:
9 x 12-inch black paper, glue, scissors, chalk, craypas, candy wrappers, sandpaper, assortment of old candies

REFERENCE:
Any art prints with trees

VOCABULARY:
Illustrator, poem, texture, relief sculpture, horizon, horizon line, intersect

ESSENTIAL QUESTIONS:
What is an illustrator?
Who writes poems and/or short stories?
What is a horizon line?
What letter is the best way to start off sketching a tree?

NATIONAL STANDARDS: 1, 2, 3, 4, 5, 6

LEARNING OBJECTIVES:
To create an illustration of a poem using mixed media.

INFORMATION:
Some artists make their careers by being "illustrators." These artists have what is called a "tight" or detailed hand. Many of them illustrate books.

Read *The Sugar Plum Tree* to students and ask them to listen with their eyes closed. Ask them to imagine the tree in their mind's eye, and to try to illustrate their vision.

Students start with a simple Y shape for the tree, using chalk to sketch, and craypas for the tree, grass, & leaves. Then they create the gingerbread dog from sandpaper and the chocolate cat from candy wrappers. Last, students add sprinkles or candies on the tree.

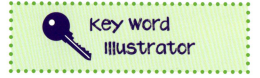

Key Word
Illustrator

STEPS:
- Sketch tree trunk and limbs with chalk
- Color the trunk and add leaves and grass with craypas
- Sketch and cut out dog and cat from sandpaper and candy wrappers
- Glue animals and candy

> **THE SUGAR-PLUM TREE,** Eugene Field (1850-1895)
>
> Have you ever heard of the Sugar-Plum Tree?
> 'Tis a marvel of great renown!
> It blooms on the shore of the Lollipop sea
> In the garden of Shut-Eye Town;
> The fruit that it bears is so wondrously sweet
> (As those who have tasted it say)
> That good little children have only to eat
> Of that fruit to be happy next day.
>
> When you've got to the tree, you would have a hard time
> To capture the fruit which I sing;
> The tree is so tall that no person could climb
> To the boughs where the sugar-plums swing!
> But up in that tree sits a chocolate cat,
> And a gingerbread dog prowls below~
> And this is the way you contrive to get at
> Those sugar-plums tempting you so:
>
> You say but the word to that gingerbread dog
> And he barks with such terrible zest
> That the chocolate cat is at once all agog,
> As her swelling proportions attest.
> And the chocolate cat goes cavorting around
> From this leafy limb unto that,
> And the sugar-plums tumble, of course, to the ground~
> Hurrah for that chocolate cat!
>
> There are marshmallows, gumdrops, and peppermint canes,
> With stripings of scarlet or gold,
> And you carry away of the treasure that rains
> As much as your apron can hold!
> So come, little child, cuddle closer to me
> In your dainty white nightcap and gown,
> And I'll rock you away to that Sugar-Plum Tree
> In the garden of Shut-Eye Town.

ARTintegration

student work

Dragon creations
Illustration/Social Studies

> **criteria:**
> - Must fill up space
> - Must use texture in dragon
> - If scale of dragon is small then add to background/negative space
> - Can add anything to negative space

ELEMENTS OF ART:
Line, Shape, Color, Value, Form, Texture, and Space

MATERIALS:
Scratch art paper, 6x9-inch yellow construction paper, glue, scratch sticks, manila paper, pencil

REFERENCE:
Chinese Dragon Robe, Japanese Dragon Scroll, laminated mythical beast reference, Eric Carle's *Dragons Dragons*

VOCABULARY:
Negative space, balance, emphasis, texture, outline, silk, dragons, emperors, weaving, embroidery, dynasty, Chinese, texture, cross-hatching, symbol, calligraphy

ESSENTIAL QUESTIONS:
What culture loves dragons?
What would be the easiest way to draw a dragon?
What textures could be used for the body?

NATIONAL STANDARDS: 1, 2, 3, 4, 5, 6

LEARNING OBJECTIVES:
To create an interesting dragon using different texture lines.

INFORMATION:
For many centuries, the Chinese kept the secret of how to raise silkworms and spin silk from the cocoons. Initially, members of the royal family spun silk for the robes that were worn to symbolize high rank. Over time, peasants were forced to raise the silkworms and weave robes for the emperor and his officials. These were especially prominent during the Qing Dynasty (1862-1974). Dragons were considered benevolent symbols of good luck, power, and rain.

Look at Chinese Dragon robes. Describe the background space. How would you describe the body of the dragon? What about the scales, spikes and whiskers? How many legs? Claws? Talons? Regular Chinese dragons had three or four claws. Five claws would signify that a robe was worn in the emperor's court.

Today we are going to create our own version of a dragon using scratch art paper. Look at reference images of mythical animals. You can use pictures as a starting point, but this dragon design must be your own. After your sketch is checked, transfer it to the black paper. Add as much texture as possible because it will allow more color to show! You may use sun, moon, clouds, stars, or calligraphy in the background so there will be lots of color and minimal negative space!

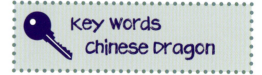

Key words
Chinese Dragon

STEPS:
- sketch on manila paper
- check
- place sketch over black paper
- trace outline of dragon
- scratch design
- mount on yellow paper

ARTintegration

student work

The Human Body & Organs
Science/Social Studies

> **Criteria:**
> - Must have main organs
> - Pay attention to scale/size of body and organs
> - Use basic shapes whenever possible

ELEMENTS OF ART:
Line, Shape, Color, Value, Form, Texture, and Space

MATERIALS:
Scissors, glue, 12 x 18-inch white construction paper, small pieces colored paper, markers, pre-cut cardboard shapes (circle, triangle, square)

REFERENCE:
George Bellows, *Dempsy and Firpo*; Pierre-Auguste Renoir, *Girl with a Watering Can*; Francisco de Goya, *Don Manuel Osorio*, Pieter Brueghel, *Wedding Dance in the Open Air*; Currier & Ives, *North American Indians*

VOCABULARY:
Organs, cells, basic shapes, proportions, tissues, systems, organic

ESSENTIAL QUESTIONS:
What shapes can be used to help you draw a realistic human body?
What are the major organs of the human body?

NATIONAL STANDARDS: 3, 4, 5, 6

LEARNING OBJECTIVES:
Students will learn how to draw the human body with correct proportions. Students will learn where the major organs of the human body are located.

INFORMATION:
The design of your body is far more sophisticated than even the most advanced computer. Billions of cells make up your body. Everyone of theses cells has special work to do for your whole body. Similar cells combine into tissues such as muscle tissue and nerve tissue. Different tissues combine into organs such as your heart and lungs. The organs combine into systems such as your skeletal system and your digestive system. The systems work in groups to serve the needs of the whole organism which is YOU!

Today we are going to use basic shapes to draw the human body. After getting a basic body shape in outline form (no body is ever really the same proportionally)…we will use the "organic shapes" to create and then locate major organs that are in the body. Let us look at some artists who painted the human body first.

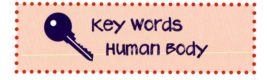
Key Words
Human Body

STEPS:
- sketch (use basic shapes/then trace around body for outline)
- draw organs
- cut
- glue

ARTintegration

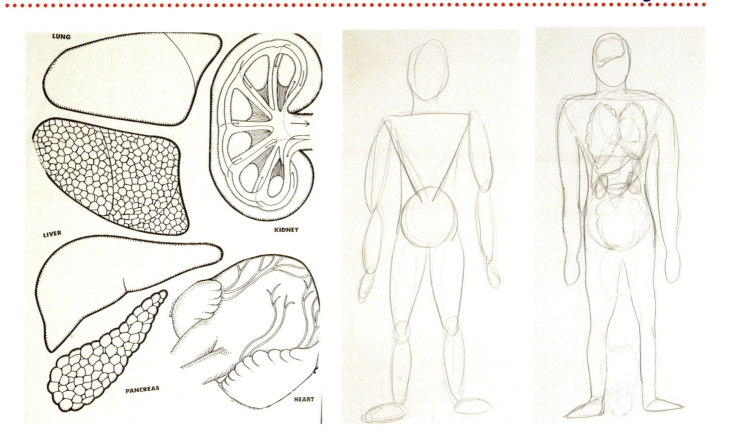

student work

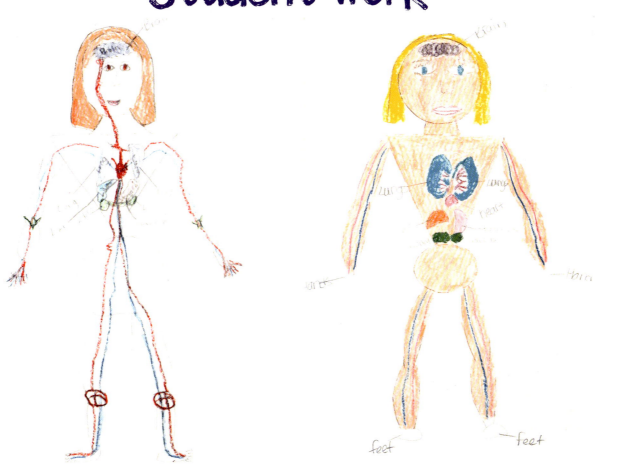

Morphed Bugs
Science/Language Arts

Criteria:
- Must take notes during video
- Creature can morph as you work
- Can use neighbor's supplies if they do not want/need them

ELEMENTS OF ART:
Line, Shape, Color, Value, Form, Texture, and Space

MATERIALS:
3 x 5-inch card, clay, half manila sheet paper, pencil, colored wires, beads, toothpicks, multicolors of modeling clay, beads, peas, acorn tops, pipecleaners, bottle caps, black eye peas, brads, cups

REFERENCE:
Bill Nye The Science Guy video on Insects, laminated pictures of bugs from National Geographic Junior calendar

VOCABULARY:
Head, thorax, abdomen, exoskeleton, eggs, larvae, pupal, adult, metamorphosis, compound eye, insect, sphere, antennae

ESSENTIAL QUESTIONS:
What are the parts of an insect?
What is its life cycle?
How do insects see?

NATIONAL STANDARDS: 1, 2, 3, 4, 5, 6

LEARNING OBJECTIVES:
Students will learn essential information about insects from watching the video. Using this knowledge, they will create the newest "classification" of bugs. Students will use available supplies to create a multi-media insect sculpture.

INFORMATION:
For an introduction, watch Bill Nye the Science Guy's Insect video. After you watch, sketch and label all of the stages and parts of insects. This will be yours to keep, and to use as reference for the newest classification of bugs that you have discovered and will sculpt out of clay. It must have eyes, antennae, legs, and abdomen (no pupa stages). Sketch your new insect before you start to sculpt.

When you finish, name (classify) your bug and write something about the bug's habitat (where it lives, what it eats).

Key word
Insect

STEPS:
- sketch on manila
- clay for abdomen & head
- add accessories!

ARTintegration

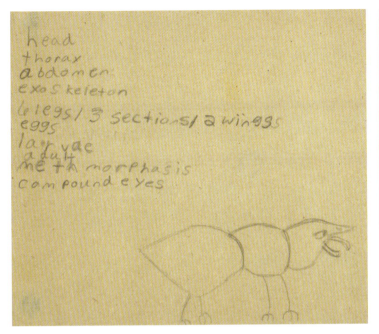

student work

Hippogriff Illustrations
Language Arts/Illustration

> **criteria:**
> - Listen to description of animal
> - Can add what isn't described
> - Fill up space (if creature is small then add to background space)

ELEMENTS OF ART:
Line, Shape, Color, Value, Form, Texture, and Space

MATERIALS:
Purple construction paper, glue, holographic/sparkle scratch paper, sticks, scrap paper, pencils

REFERENCE:
Images of mythical creatures, *Harry Potter and the Prisoner of Azkaban*

VOCABULARY:
Illustrator, transfer, trace, mythology, wizard, orphan, author, crosshatching, stippling, publisher, creature, imagination.

ESSENTIAL QUESTIONS:
What does an author do? What does an illustrator do? What does imagination mean?

NATIONAL STANDARDS: 2, 3, 4, 5, 6

LEARNING OBJECTIVES:
Students will learn about a career as an illustrator. They will be illustrators and draw their version of a creature from *Harry Potter and The Prisoner of Azkaban*.

INFORMATION:
Some artists make their careers by being illustrators. Most of them illustrate books, but brochures, magazines, and posters are a few other areas where they would be needed. Show samples of a variety of illustrations.

Have any of you read any Harry Potter books? The stories are about an orphan boy who lives with his wretched aunt and uncle until acceptance into Hogwarts School of Witchcraft and Wizardry changes his life forever. I became interested in the illustrator when I saw the book covers. Although there are only small illustrations inside the books, these and the book covers were done by Mary GrandPré. Then I found an article that told how she received her inspiration. She was on a tight deadline for the first book, so she used what she had available to sketch from — herself! Artists do this all the time!

Today you will illustrate your version of a creature from *Harry Potter and The Prisoner of Azkaban*. There is no right or wrong way to draw this creature. Refer to the reference images and remember to use basic shapes for the animal. After your sketch is checked, place it over the black glitter scratch paper and retrace the outline. Add stars, moons, asteroids or anything else that you would like in the background or negative space.

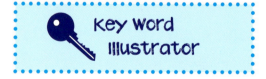
Key word Illustrator

STEPS:
- sketch
- trace
- scratch (try different techniques)
- mount on purple construction paper

ARTintegration

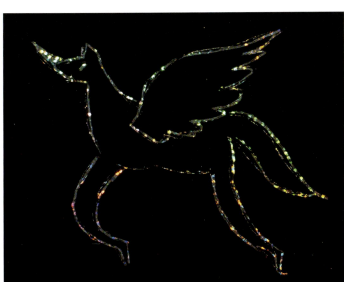

student work

Mexican Woven Cloth
Social Studies/Math/Textile Design

Criteria:
- can be all shapes or animals and shapes
- can be any scale/size
- must be scratched with textures

ELEMENTS OF ART:
Line, Shape, Color, Value, Form, Texture, and Space

MATERIALS:
Black scratch art paper (quarter of sheet), 6 x 9-inch yellow construction paper, pencil, manila scrap paper, scratch sticks, rulers

REFERENCE:
Woven belts, serapes, blankets, and purses from Mexico

VOCABULARY:
Textile, woven, cloth, design, functional, secular, sacred, loom, costume

ESSENTIAL QUESTIONS:
What does textile mean?
What type of textiles are from Mexico?
How do you weave cloth?

NATIONAL STANDARDS: 1, 2, 3, 4, 5, 6

LEARNING OBJECTIVES:
To create a design inspired by Mexican weavings using scratch art paper. Students will simulate the look of woven cloth.

INFORMATION:
Textile skills in Mexico are focused mainly on the creation of clothing. Throughout its long history, Mexican costume has evolved absorbing new features and keeping many elements of Pre-Hispanic dress. In their contemporary textiles, you can see a fusion of different materials, garment styles, and decorative images.

Today, most articles of clothing are woven on a loom. Woven textiles are made by interlacing one series of threads, known as the "weft," with a second series of threads called "warp."

In many indigenous societies, it is impossible to separate the secular from the sacred. Among the Huichol people of Mexico, clothing has a spiritual as well as functional role. The designs in the cloth serve as visual prayers meant to protect the wearer from harm. They carry many layers of meanings. One example is the long, winding serpent shapes which serve as requests for rain. The rain in turn brings good crops, health, and long life. Color and design motifs also have symbolic importance in the Chiapas Highlands and in parts of Oaxaca. The designs on sashes are believed to guard unborn children against evil forces. Women labor long hours to clothe themselves and their families. They take great pride in their skill. Using simple animal shapes, lines and textures, we will create the look of a woven cloth.

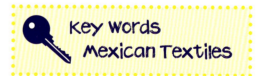

Key Words
Mexican Textiles

STEPS:
- sketch on manila (outline of shapes/straight lines with rulers)
- check
- place manila over scratch art
- trace design with short lines
- mount

ARTintegration

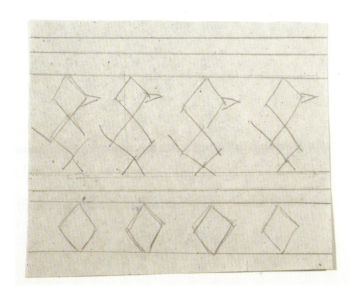
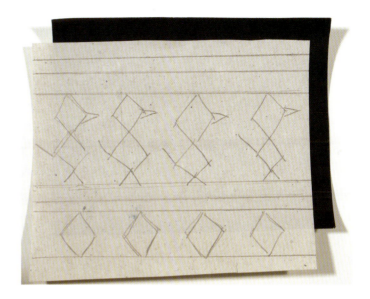

student work

29

Arcs & Protractors
Math/Social Studies

criteria:
- Must overlap tools
- New shapes – different colors
- Show value scale in shapes

ELEMENTS OF ART:
Line, Shape, Color, Value, Form, Texture, and Space

MATERIALS:
White construction paper, protractors, French curves, compasses, circles, watercolor pencils, cups, brushes

REFERENCE:
Sonia Delaunay, *Electrical Prisms & Peinture N 123-A*; MacDonald Wright, *Airplane Synchromy in Yellow-Orange*, Frank Stella, *Darabjerd III*

VOCABULARY:
Protractor, compass, arc, design, pattern, nonobjective, tint, value

ESSENTIAL QUESTIONS:
What is an arc?
What is a protractor used for?
What is a compass used for?

NATIONAL STANDARDS: 1, 2, 3, 5, 6

LEARNING OBJECTIVES:
Students will learn how to measure acute, right, and obtuse angles. They will create a design by overlapping tools that are used to make arcs. They will use the value scale and create tints within each shape.

INFORMATION:
SONIA DELAUNAY (1885-1979)
- born in Russia; moved to Paris
- worked only with color and abstract shapes
- designed unique fabrics after a pieced blanket sewn for her first child
- designed stage sets and costumes for ballet and theatre

MACDONALD WRIGHT (1890-1973)
- born in Charlottesville, Virginia
- went to Paris at 17 to study Art (Fauvism, Futurism, color, abstractions)
- co-founder of Synchronism — style with free-flowing, vivid color patterns
- exhibited in Armory Show in 1913 and Alfred Steiglitz's 291 Gallery in 1917
- taught at the University of California and wrote articles on color

FRANK STELLA (born 1936)
- nonobjective paintings using huge, unusually shaped canvases
- created a series of protractor paintings… taped off areas to create a "hard" edge for the paint
- used bright, bold colors

Today you will create your own design using protractors and French curves. Remember that artists are always looking for new and different ways to create art. Always try something new when creating. Don't be afraid to experiment — even mistakes might create something wonderful.

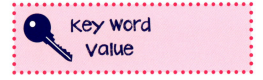
Key word
Value

STEPS:
- sketch
- watercolor pencils (light to dark values)
- use brush to add water and blend color

ALTERNATE LESSON PLAN (3-5): Use protractors with math criteria (angles) first — students measure right angle, an acute angle, and an obtuse angle drawn on board.

ARTintegration

student work

Crazy Quilts
Social Studies/Math/Textile Design

Criteria:
- Must use a variety of textures and shapes
- Use one or more crayons in shapes of color
- Use light watercolor wash for resist

ELEMENTS OF ART:
Line, Shape, Color, Value, Form, Texture, and Space

MATERIALS:
Half of white construction paper, watercolor paints, paper towels, brushes, pencil, crayons

REFERENCE:
Old quilts or photographs of quilts

VOCABULARY:
Translucent, resist, colonial, embroidery, 1775-1875, quilt, patchwork, pattern, appliqué, crazy quilt, triangle, hexagon

ESSENTIAL QUESTIONS:
What are the names of the early quilt patterns? How are they made?
What shapes are used in the patterns of the patchwork quilts?
What is embroidery?

NATIONAL STANDARDS: 1, 2, 3, 4, 5, 6

LEARNING OBJECTIVES:
Students will create a crazy quilt pattern using simple shapes. They will uses a crayon/watercolor resist technique.

INFORMATION:
Layers of fabric have been used for centuries as a way of protecting and insulating the human body. Quilting has been traced back as far as the Middle Ages. In Southern Europe, where it was warmer, quilting became decorative art for clothing. In Northern Europe, quilting provided protection from the cold weather. It was used in clothing and to cover the bed. Quilting became valuable because of the intricate and decorative embroidery stitches that fastened layers of cloth together. Quilts were prized family possessions and were passed down though the generations. In colonial America, quilts were brought over by the Pilgrim families. As the quilts wore out, they were carefully patched with any type of fabric that was available. Early designs were based on repetitive geometric shapes and had symbolic ties. More intricate patterns were floral and animal fabric shapes applied on top of the quilted squares. All of the layers of fabric were held together by rows of strong, tiny stitches. The stitches created patterns on top of the cloth too. By the 18th & 19th centuries, American patchwork quilts were developed more extensively. The patchwork quilt became a record of family history because old clothing was recycled and used as the fabric for quilts. It also became an important part of pioneer social life. It was common for friends to gather to socialize and stitch.

Students will create a version of a quilt pattern using a crayon/watercolor resist process.

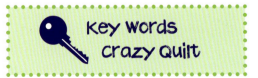
Key Words
Crazy Quilt

STEPS:
- sketch
- crayon
- watercolor paint (use light-dark)

ARTintegration

student work

33

Dynamic Diamonds
Math/Social Studies

> **Criteria:**
> - Make good use of positive and negative space
> - Can use any colors
> - Must have some 3D shapes

ELEMENTS OF ART:
Line, Shape, Color, Value, Form, Texture, and Space

MATERIALS:
White construction paper, pencils, glue, recycled triangle paper scraps

REFERENCE:
Sonia Delaunay, *Electrical Prisms* and *Peinture N 123-A*, MacDonald Wright, *Airplane Synchromy in Yellow-Orange*, Frank Stella, *Darabjerd III*, and Marilyn Burns, *The Greedy Triangle* (book)

VOCABULARY:
Abstract, triangle, diamonds, angles, relief sculpture, geometric, intersecting, hard-edged, adjacent, warm/cool colors

ESSENTIAL QUESTIONS:
What does abstract mean?
What is a "relief" sculpture?
What geometric shapes do you know?

NATIONAL STANDARDS: 1, 2, 4, 5, 6

LEARNING OBJECTIVES:
Students will learn to identify all of the geometric shapes. They will create a relief sculpture using recycled paper triangles.

INFORMATION:

SONIA DELAUNAY (1885-1979)
- born in Russia, moved to Paris
- she and her husband, Robert, worked only with color and shape in revolutionary style called Abstract Expressionism
- designed unique fabrics after a pieced blanket sewn for her first child
- designed stage sets and costume design for ballet & theatre

MACDONALD WRIGHT (1890-1973)
- born in Charlottesville, Virginia
- went to Paris at age 17 in 1907 to study Art (Fauvism, Futurism, color abstractions)
- He and Morgan Russell became co-founders of Synchronism, a style based on free-flowing, vivid color patterns
- exhibited in Armory Show in 1913 & Stieglitz's (NY) in 1917
- taught at the University of California
- author of several articles on color

WASSILY KANDINSKY (1866-1944)
- first artist to abandon representation of objects in painting
- part of Der Blaue Reiter, a group of artists that chose to paint this way
- painter gave thrill not able to get in nature

Today we will create some abstract artwork using shapes like these artists did. We will also be recycling supplies from a mask project from last year. You may create other shapes and 3-D forms as you work.

Key Word
Relief Surface

STEPS:
- layout
- glue

ARTintegration

student work

Dots Forever
Math/Textile Design

CRITERIA:
- Must fold at least four times
- Must use Q-tips; straw is optional
- Colors must repeat

ELEMENTS OF ART:
Line, Shape, Color, Value, Form, Texture, and Space

MATERIALS:
Yellow construction paper, pencils, straws, Q-tips, paint caps (paint by number containers)

REFERENCE:
Examples of textile design wrapping papers and cloths

VOCABULARY:
Repeat pattern, block, apparel, design, printmaking, diagonal, vertical, horizontal

ESSENTIAL QUESTIONS:
What is a pattern?
What is a stripe?
What is a plaid?

NATIONAL STANDARDS: 1, 2, 4, 5, 6

LEARNING OBJECTIVES:
Students will learn to identify repeat patterns. They will create a simple dot repeat pattern using 3-6 colors of paint.

INFORMATION:
At one time, we worked on a name project that involved a random type of patterning. Depending on how many letters were in your name, your pattern appeared to be a stripe, diagonal, or another interesting type of pattern. In design, whether it is for wallpaper, wrapping paper, domestic textiles, or apparel, there are 2 basic repeat patterns. One is a block pattern where a unit of some dimension is repeated over and over again in a way that resembles stacked blocks or cubes (show examples).

The other type of repeat is when the block is moved over half-way on the row below, called a half-drop. The advantage of this type of repetition is to allow for variation in your design. It doesn't read as set or static and usually makes the pattern appear larger (show examples). We will use Q-tips & straws to create a repeat pattern. Take your time planning the colors and their placement because the process goes quickly and you need to concentrate on your design.

Key Word
Repeat Pattern

STEPS:
- fold paper four times
- paint light to dark colors

ARTintegration

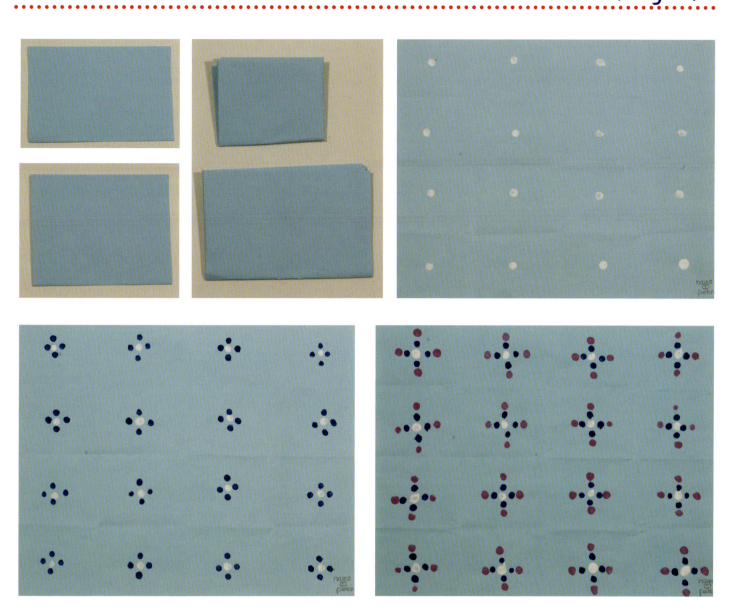

student work

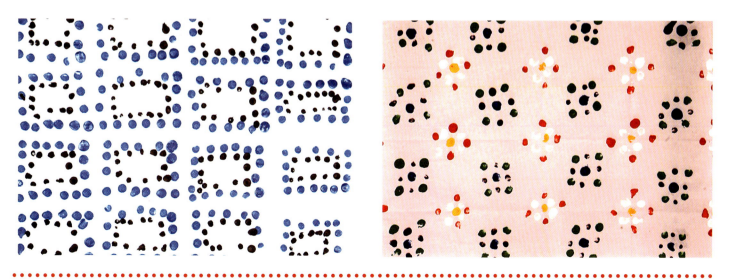

Gingerbread Houses
Math/Language Arts/Architecture

> **Criteria:**
> - Must have horizon line
> - Can have any amount of snow
> - Use variety of candy color/texture

ELEMENTS OF ART:
Line, Shape, Color, Value, Form, Texture, and Space

MATERIALS:
Light blue construction paper, pencils, crayons, rulers, cut squares, triangles, assorted candies & decorator "doodads", detergent, cups, glue

REFERENCE:
Examples of different pictures/gift boxes of the witch's house that Hansel and Gretel found.

VOCABULARY:
Illustrator, shapes, parallel, horizon, cube, rectangular solid, relief surface, architecture, texture, angle, parallelogram, highlights

ESSENTIAL QUESTIONS:
What is a parallelogram?
What basic shapes do you need to draw a house?
What is a horizon line?
What is a rectangular solid?

NATIONAL STANDARDS: 1, 2, 4, 5, 6

LEARNING OBJECTIVES:
Students will learn to use the geometric shapes to create a realistic house. They will create a relief gingerbread house using mixed media.

INFORMATION:
Every project in this book has stressed the use of simple and/or basic shapes. Using these shapes, whether drawing buildings, leaves, fruit, or animals will increase the realism of the object that you are drawing. Several of the projects also had a theme of architecture. This project will be the culmination and combining of all of the skills we have learned. In addition to your use of all of the elements of art, you will use the parallelogram for this project. This will introduce a third dimension (perspective) to your buildings and make them look more realistic. (Demonstrate parallelogram and its use in architecture)

In the story of Hansel and Gretel, they find a house in the woods "made of cake and the windows of sugar." Each book has a slightly different version, but very little description, leaving illustrators plenty of leeway when creating their version of the house. Gingerbread houses have become a popular tradition for many during the holidays or for special occasions.

Today we will create a version of the "cottage" with whatever types of candies, cookies etc. you wish to add to yours. There is detergent for icing, snow or clouds. When you finish, you can add some decorator candies to your house too.

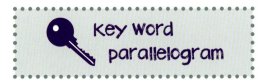

Key word parallelogram

STEPS:
- sketch (horizon line/building/trees/candies, and cookies)
- color with crayon
- add candies
- glue snow/icing/clouds
- glue candies

ARTintegration

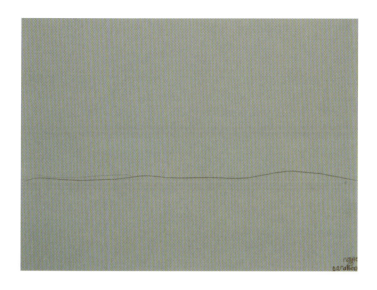
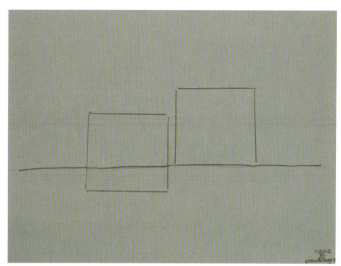
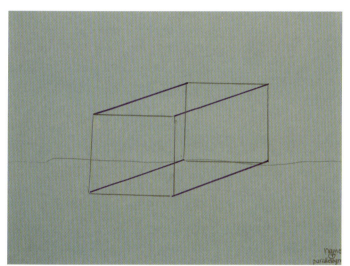
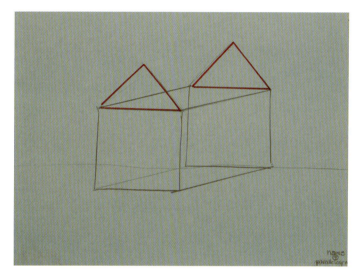

student work

Paisley Power
Social Studies/Math/Textile Design

criteria:
- can use reference but must change scale
- Must have at least 1 large and 1 small paisley
- can be floral, geometric, or both

ELEMENTS OF ART:
Line, Shape, Color, Value, Form, Texture, and Space

MATERIALS:
Scratch art fluorescent papers (cut in 4ths), manila paper, pencils, half sheet of white construction paper, glue

REFERENCE:
Examples of different wrapping paper and textile paisley designs and patterns, laminated paisley reference sheets, map (for countries), men's ties

VOCABULARY:
paisley, texture, floral, decorative, curvy, organic, fluorescent, motif, woven

ESSENTIAL QUESTIONS:
What is paisley?
Describe what it looks like?
What does decorative mean?

NATIONAL STANDARDS: 1, 2, 3, 4, 5, 6

LEARNING OBJECTIVES:
Students will learn the history of the paisley motif. They will create a design using simple shapes and flowers and use scratch art paper.

INFORMATION:
Paisley, with its familiar teardrop motif, carries the name of the Scottish town that produced woven paisley shawls beginning in the first decade of the 19th century. But the town of Paisley was not the only, or even the first, center for making and marketing paisley textiles. In Norwich and Edinburgh (as in Paris and Vienna), manufacturers produced designs "in imitation of the Indian" as early as 1780. India was where the paisley shape had survived since before the Roman Empire. By late 17th century, it was widely used there on decorative shawls. Rooted in traditional Indian floral designs, the paisley motif was called the "Kashmir Cone," or the teardrop, mango, tadpole, or pine tree. The form was abstracted from the growing shoot of the date palm tree (the legendary tree of life) which originated in prehistoric Babylon and spread into ancient Europe and India.

Today we are going to look at and compare some of the examples of paisley used in textiles (ties, shirts) and wrapping papers. We will then create simple paisley images focusing on the line and texture on scratch art fluorescent paper.

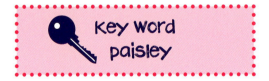
Key word paisley

STEPS:
- sketch (on manila)
- check
- retrace manila on top of scratch
- scratch out
- mount on white

ARTintegration

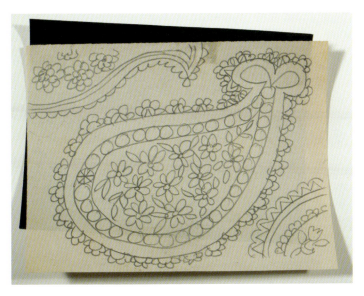
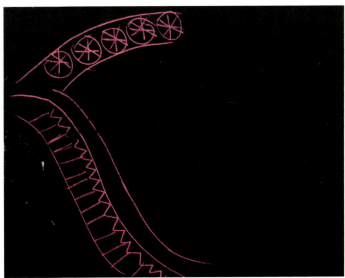

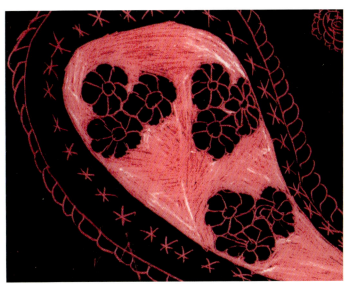

student work

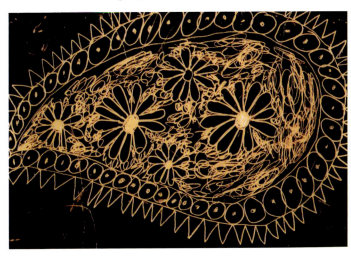

Angel Wrap
Social Studies/Math/Design

> **Criteria:**
> - Must be a repeat pattern
> - Can use glitter in other places
> - Can add other art mediums

ELEMENTS OF ART:
Line, Shape, Color, Value, Form, Texture, and Space

MATERIALS:
Blue bulletin board paper, potatoes, knife, glue, glitter, white paint, paper plates

REFERENCE:
Examples of different wrapping paper patterns

VOCABULARY:
print, design, holiday, festival, celebration, solstice, pattern

ESSENTIAL QUESTIONS:
What does solstice mean?
What is a symbol?
What is a pattern?

NATIONAL STANDARDS: 1, 2, 4, 5, 6

LEARNING OBJECTIVES:
Students will review different types of repeat patterns. They will create their own pattern for gift wrap for presents. Students will learn a basic printmaking technique.

INFORMATION:
Angels have been depicted in Hindu, Jewish, Islamic, Egyptian, African and countless other cultural/religious groups. Throughout the centuries these messengers from the Heavens have always been protectors or symbols of love and goodness.

We are going to create simple designs for printing some gift wrap today that can be used to celebrate the holidays. All cultures and religions have some celebration involving light or a festival of lights at this time of year. Early people were very in tune with the earth, stars and nature….and welcomed the return of the "sun."

Key Word: Pattern

STEPS:
- mark rows (with pencil)
- paint potato
- print potato
- sketch halo
- glue
- glitter

ARTintegration

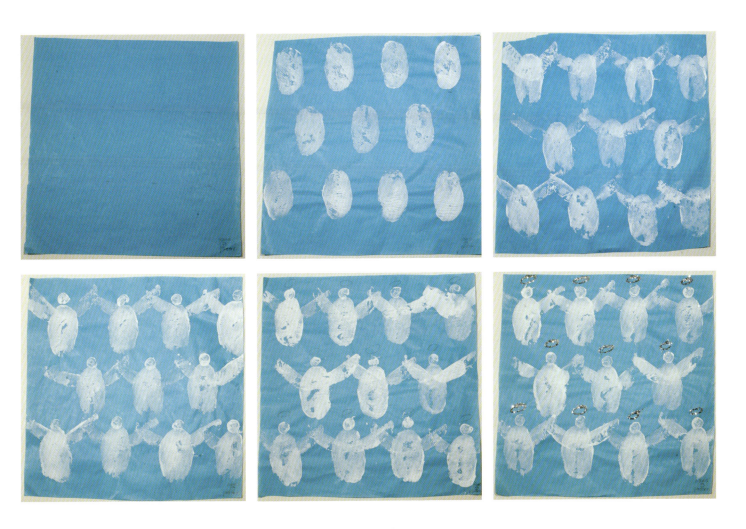

student work

43

Personal Cartouche
Social Studies/Language Arts/Art

Criteria:
- Use name in hieroglyphics
- Can use nickname
- Must use space of paper

ELEMENTS OF ART:
Line, Shape, Color, Value, Form, Texture, and Space

MATERIALS:
Hot dog paper holder, pencil, black marker, black pen, beige pastels, scissors, pencil

REFERENCE:
Pictures of hieroglyphics, Ancient Egyptian Wall Painting: *Pashedu with the Sacred Eye of Horus, Presentation of the Cup*

VOCABULARY:
Egyptian, cartouche, hieroglyphics, pyramid, Africa, tomb, Rosetta Stone, civilization, monument, papyrus

ESSENTIAL QUESTIONS:
Who were the Egyptians?
When did they live? Where did they live?
What was their picture language called?
What is a cartouche?

NATIONAL STANDARDS: 1, 2, 4, 5, 6

LEARNING OBJECTIVES:
Students will learn to use hieroglyphics for their names while creating a cartouche like the kings of Egypt used.

INFORMATION:
Egypt is a country in northeast Africa. It was here, over 5,000 years ago, that the pyramids were constructed. For thousands of years, they were the largest structures in the world. Even now, archeologists are still collecting information as to how they were built.

The Egyptians also invented one of the very first written languages, a picture language of beautifully drawn birds and animals, called hieroglyphics. The word comes from the ancient Greeks and means "sacred carving."

In 1799, a small slab of stone was found at the mouth of the Nile near the town of Rosetta. The same message was carved in different languages. One was ancient Greek which we could read and one was hieroglyphics. Two great scholars, Thomas Young and Jean Francois Champollion studied the stone in an attempt to decipher it or break the code. They discovered that hieroglyphics contained in a rope loop (cartouche) were the names of pharaohs. By comparing the names of the Greek rulers, Ptolemy and Cleopatra to the hieroglyphs in the cartouche, they discovered that each stood for a sound. Champollion went on to crack the code and in 1832 his work was published. (Explain how sounds work)

Today we will create our own cartouche just as the kings had with their names in them. Using the reference chart to draw from, we will use large hot dog papers to create the cartouche.

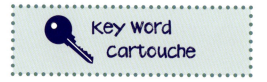
Key word cartouche

STEPS:
- trace stencil of cartouche (or draw your own)
- sketch border
- letters
- colored pencils/pastels
- cut

ARTintegration

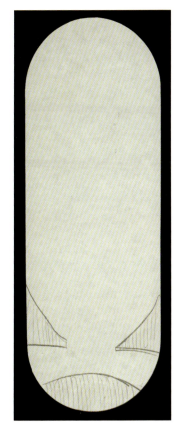  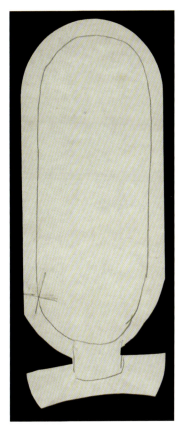 

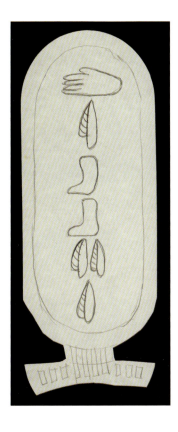 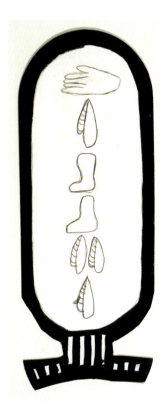 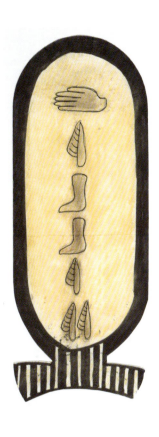

student work

Santa Paint Sticks
Social Studies/Language Arts/Crafts

> **Criteria:**
> - Must paint light to dark
> - Must rinse brush well between colors
> - Can use thin markers for facial features

ELEMENTS OF ART:
Line, Shape, Color, Value, Form, Texture, and Space

MATERIALS:
12-inch stick, red, white, beige & black paint, cups, brushes, paper towels, newspaper, pencils

REFERENCE:
Pictures of Santa Claus

VOCABULARY:
illustrator, poem, dowry, Bavarian, imagination, visualize, found object, recycle

ESSENTIAL QUESTIONS:
What is an author?
What is an illustrator?
Do you know where most of our Christmas traditions come from?

NATIONAL STANDARDS: 1, 2, 3, 4, 5, 6

LEARNING OBJECTIVES:
Students will use a found "stick" to create a Santa Claus sculpture.

INFORMATION:
Children the world over know and love St. Nicholas. He is known as the patron saint of children. Legends of his goodness began years ago when he helped three girls who needed dowries by throwing sacks of gold down their chimney. Over the years, he has been called many names and has dressed in many different outfits.

Children in America know him as Santa Claus. When the Dutch settlers arrived in America, they changed the Dutch name Sant Nikolass to Santa Claus. But this was still not the fellow we know today. Two Americans, Thomas Nast and Clement C. Moore are credited with this. Clement's poem "A Visit from St. Nicholas" or "The Night Before Christmas", written in 1822, pictured Santa as a chubby, pipe-smoking, jolly fellow. He also introduced the idea of St. Nick riding a reindeer. Thomas Nast, a cartoonist for Harper's Weekly, drew the cartoons from 1863-1866 which caricaured St. Nicholas as the Santa Claus we know today. In some of the early pictures, Santa Claus almost looks "gnome-like" and has German style whiskers. In his hat, a sprig of holly and mistletoe was placed which is a remnant of an ancient wreath.

Today you will use your imagination to create Santa out of a paint stick. You must be able to visualize where his face is first...followed by hat/body/legs etc.

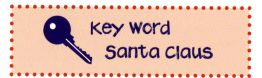

Key word
Santa Claus

STEPS:
- sketch face, hat & belt
- paint white
- paint beige
- paint red
- paint black
- rinse brush and water cup

ARTintegration

student work

47

Pennsylvania Dutch Folk Art
Social Studies/Art

> **Criteria:**
> - Must use all space of paper plate
> - Must use variation of fraktur designs
> - Must use color available

ELEMENTS OF ART:
Line, Shape, Color, Value, Form, Texture, and Space

MATERIALS:
Red/black crayons, paint, sponges, paper plates, pencils, small plates

REFERENCE:
Examples of Pennsylvania Dutch Hex signs, fraktur reference sheets

VOCABULARY:
Fraktur, hex sign, Pennsylvania Dutch, graffito, glaze, transparent, inhabitants, emigrants, settlers, design

ESSENTIAL QUESTIONS:
Who were the Pennsylvania Dutch?
What does Fraktur mean?

NATIONAL STANDARDS: 1, 2, 3, 4, 5, 6

LEARNING OBJECTIVES:
Students will create their version of a fraktur on a paper plate. They will use fraktur "designs" to modify or create their own.

INFORMATION:
George Habener was part of a successful community of settlers who became known as the Pennsylvania Dutch. They were emigrants from Germanic sections of Central Europe. "Dutch" was a corrupted word that the English had to refer to inhabitants of Germany. "Deutsch" means German.

Southeastern Pennsylvania was rich in ceramic-quality clay deposits. They were just beneath a rich topsoil, near rivers and streams in low-lying areas. The excellent farms and active potteries were possible because of the soil. And the abundance of firewood for stoking the kilns added to the development of the local pottery industry.

Sgraffito designs were originally found almost exclusively among the Pennsylvania Dutch (sgraffito comes from an Italian word meaning to scratch). Once the designs were complete, the plate was covered with a transparent glaze. A yellowish cast was given to the glaze by the addition of iron oxide, and the browns and greens were created by applying small amounts of the glaze containing manganese and copper oxide. Earthenware was waterproofed with lead glazes. The poisonous nature of lead caused sickness in the potters, as well as in those who ate from the ware.

These plates were given for special occasions such as births, marriages, or visits from the distant relatives. This was also done on paper, and the designs are called Frakturs.

Fraktur comes from the 16th century German type-style comprised of thin shapes, pointed ends and bristling serifs. The most popular designs were hearts, tulips pomegranates, birds, unicorns, angels, and fanciful creatures.

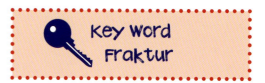
Key word Fraktur

STEPS:
- sketch
- crayon
- dab paint

ARTintegration

student work

49

Thayer: Father of Camouflage

Science/Art/Language Arts

> **Criteria:**
> - Must use chameleon (can draw your own if desired)
> - Must glue chameleon near several colors
> - Match color values

ELEMENTS OF ART:
Line, Shape, Color, Value, Form, Texture & Space

MATERIALS:
Wallpaper pieces, scissors, chameleon print, glue, pencil, oil pastels

REFERENCE:
A Color of His Own by Leo Lionni, examples of Thayer's artwork from Art Activities #

VOCABULARY:
Camouflage, color, coloration, coloring, contour, blend, shading, theory, pattern, outline, tints, shades

ESSENTIAL QUESTIONS:
What does camouflage mean?
Why does nature camouflage animals?
How do we blend colors?

NATIONAL STANDARDS: 1, 2, 3, 4, 5, 6

LEARNING OBJECTIVES:
Students will try to camouflage chameleons on patterned wallpaper sheets. They will match the tints and shades of the colors where they have placed the paper chameleon.

INFORMATION:
A painter of angels, Abbott Thayer became the father of camouflage in the United States at the turn of the 19th century. He was born in New Hampshire and loved birds and collected animal skins. While at a prep school in Boston, he studied with an animal painter. He sold paintings of birds and animals while he attended the National Academy of Design in New York. He married, studied art in Paris, and then moved back to the United States. He did commissioned portraits to support his family, but soon was outside painting animals. He developed a theory of "protective coloration" based on blending, disruption (strong arbitrary patterns of color flatten contours and break up outlines) and counter-shading (animals having darkest colors on top where light hits/lightest underneath).

Thayer tried to sell his camouflage ideas during World War I, but he died before most of his ideas were really used. Nowadays, camouflage is well accepted in the field of science and is used for the military.

Today I am going to share a book about an animal that knows how to camouflage....a chameleon! (Read book.) You will draw and cut out a chameleon and then try to "camouflage" it on a piece of printed wallpaper with oil pastels.

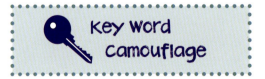

Key Word Camouflage

STEPS:
- draw and cut out chameleon shape
- glue on wallpaper background
- color with craypas

ARTintegration

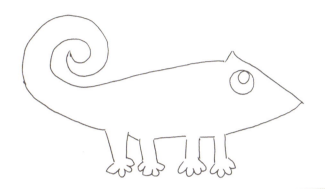
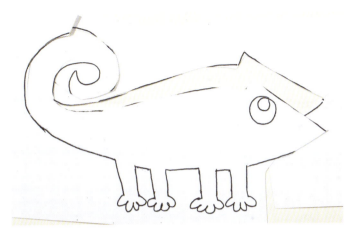

student work

Pueblo Tale
Design/Social Studies/Language Arts/Math

> **criteria:**
> - Must illustrate the boy
> - Can add background and border design
> - Must use lots of texture

ELEMENTS OF ART:
Line, Shape, Color, Value, Form, Texture, and Space

MATERIALS:
Yellow construction paper, multi-scratch art paper (cut in 4ths), pencils, sticks, glue, scrap paper (same size as scratch paper)

REFERENCE:
Native American Indian patterns (wrapping paper, fabric), *Arrow to the Sun* by Gerald McDermott

VOCABULARY:
Pueblo, tale, illustrator, myth, legend, worship, kachina, culture

ESSENTIAL QUESTIONS:
Who were the Pueblo Indians?
What is a tale?
Who are Kachinas?

NATIONAL STANDARDS: 1, 2, 3, 4, 5, 6

LEARNING OBJECTIVES:
Students will work as illustrators do. They will create their own version of the boy from the story. Students will use technique of scratch art paper.

INFORMATION:
For the past weeks, we have been exploring all different types of literature from illuminated manuscripts to myths and legends. Today you will be illustrators (someone who does the artwork from a story in a book) for a Pueblo Indian tale. The story is called *Arrow to the Sun*. When I read this story I want you to be thinking about kachinas we made last semester with the glitter crayons and feathers. (Ask what a kachina is?) In Pueblo culture, the kachina are divine spirits who act as intermediaries between man and God. The kachina are never worshiped, but are thought of as benevolent spirits and friends. They are named according to what they represent, usually animals, crops or human attributes. Read story to students.

When you draw your version of the boy, use simple, basic shapes for the body and the face. Sketch on the manila scrap paper.... add sky, rainbow etc. When the picture is ready for transfer...place sketch on top of the scratch art paper and press down to retrace what you have drawn. Then lift off the scrap piece of paper and use scratch stick to draw textures and shapes. Avoid touching the scratch paper as much as possible (the oils in you hands will keep the black from scratching off). Then mount it on the yellow sheet on paper.

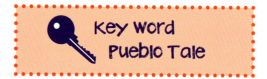

Key word
Pueblo Tale

STEPS:
- sketch on manila
- retrace drawing (manila on top of scratch paper)
- use stick to scratch out illustration

ALTERNATE LESSON PLAN (3-5):
Use grid paper and colored pencils. Some students chose to only work with black.

ARTintegration

student work

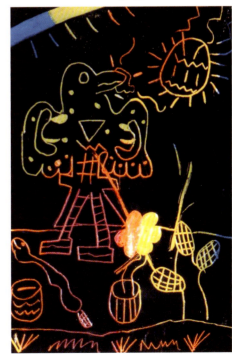

Contemporary Sculptures
Art/Social Studies/Math

> **Criteria:**
> - Use organic or geometric shapes
> - Must be 3D in some way
> - Must use lots of color
> - Must work on both sides of sculpture

ELEMENTS OF ART:
Line, Shape, Color, Value, Form, Texture, and Space

MATERIALS:
5 x 18-inch white construction paper, pencil, markers, scissors, ruler

REFERENCE:
John McCracken, Hayden Williams, Dorothy Gillespie

VOCABULARY:
Sculpture, contemporary, designer, print, fabric, "happening" complementary, optical, form, 3-D, illusion, organic, geometric

ESSENTIAL QUESTIONS:
What is a sculpture?
What media can be used to make sculptures?
What does contemporary mean?

NATIONAL STANDARDS: 1, 2, 3, 4, 5, 6

LEARNING OBJECTIVES:
Students will work in the style of Dorothy Gillespie creating a three-dimensional form.

INFORMATION:

JOHN MCCRACKEN (born 1943)
- *Manchu* is a wood, fiberglass, and lacquer sculpture
- controls perception of mass with color (make heavy form appear lighter)
- High key colors emphasize three-dimensionality. Complementary colors reinforce the effect of expansion.

HAYDEN WILLIAMS (born 1991)
- *Extension* is a cotton print fabric
- fabric designers create on a flat surface — will suggest depth or create optical illusions by carefully arranging elements
- if the fabric is gathered into folds — instead of destroying the pattern — the changing depth shows 3D effects of color and form

DOROTHY GILLESPIE (1921-2002)
- born in Roanoke, Virginia. Went to Maryland Institute College of Art, then moved to NYC
- Rituals '71 was a "Happening" for 3 hours one Sunday afternoon. She painted on enormous sheets of paper continued to create works on massive sheets of paper
- fought for Woman's Arts Rights
- loved public work commissions because she believed art should be accessible to large audiences

Today we will create a sculpture similar to one of Gillespie's earlier paper sculptures. You will need colorful shapes (organic or geometric) and markers. When you have cut your strips, you may curl them or bend them to suit yourself. Be sure to work on both sides of the paper!

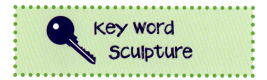

Key word
Sculpture

STEPS:
- sketch
- color with markers
- cut
- curl

ARTintegration

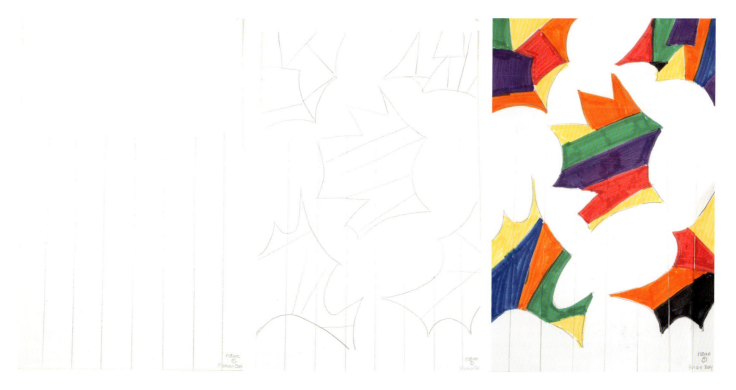

student work

Mondrian/Nonobjective Art
Art/Math

> **criteria:**
> - Paint "flat"
> - Measure lines of shapes
> - Must use one shape each of primary colors

ELEMENTS OF ART:
Line, Shape, Color, Value, Form, Texture, and Space

MATERIALS:
9 x 18-inch white construction paper, pencil, black floor tape, ruler, red/blue/yellow paint, brushes, paper towels, cups

REFERENCE:
Frank Stella, Piet Mondrian, Josef Albers

VOCABULARY:
Nonobjective, primary, secondary, parallel, perpendicular, squares, rectangles

ESSENTIAL QUESTIONS:
What does Nonobjective mean?
What are the primary colors?
Why do you think artists would want to paint this way?

NATIONAL STANDARDS: 1, 2, 3, 4, 5, 6

LEARNING OBJECTIVES:
Students will create a nonobjective design in the style of Mondrian using primary colors and basic shapes. They will learn how to measure with rulers.

INFORMATION:
FRANK STELLA (born 1936)
- non-objective paintings using huge shaped canvases
- did whole set of protractor series....taped off areas on canvas to have the paint have a hard edge
- bright, bold colors....sometimes used household paints

PIET MONDRIAN (1872-1944)
- principle artist responsible for 20th century nonobjective paintings
- born in Holland—studied at the academy and was influenced by Cubism (faceted planes)
- group called the "De Stijl" wanted art to be universal and independent from emotions
- primary colors/vertical and horizontal bands

JOSEF ALBERS (1888-1976)
- color and light studies were his main focus
- German born, settled in the United States
- did series of paintings/color studies called "Homage to the Square"

Today we will create some nonobjective art in the style of Mondrian. Remember to paint as flat as you possibly can...very, very little texture!

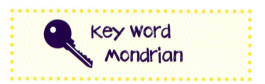

Key word: Mondrian

STEPS:
- draw/measure lines
- tape
- paint yellow/red/blue

ALTERNATE PROJECT (3-5):
Use the secondary color floor tapes with rectangles, squares & triangles.

ALTERNATE PROJECT (K-2):
Enlarge sheet from a crossword puzzle and have students use primary-colored markers to create a design.

ARTintegration

student work

Lineamaniacs
Math/Design/Social Studies

> **Criteria:**
> - Must have parallel lines
> - Use intersecting lines
> - Must overlap lines

ELEMENTS OF ART:
Line, Shape, Color, Value, Form, Texture, and Space

MATERIALS:
9 x 12-inch black construction paper, pencil, glue, scissors, markers, recycled shredded strips of typing paper

REFERENCE:
Jackson Pollock, Victor Vasarely, Kenneth Noland

VOCABULARY:
Line, parallel, intersecting, overlap, abstract, composition, texture, kinetic, optic, vibration

ESSENTIAL QUESTIONS:
What does Abstract mean?
What are intersecting lines?
What are parallel lines?
What does overlap mean?
What does kinetic mean?

NATIONAL STANDARDS: 1, 2, 3, 4, 5, 6

LEARNING OBJECTIVES:
Students will create an abstract composition using recycled paper strips. They can use color on the strips (lines) and must fill up their space.

INFORMATION:

JACKSON POLLOCK (1912-1956)
- born in Wyoming, USA
- part of Roosevelt's WPA Federal Art Program which gave financial support to artists during the Depression.
- influenced by Picasso…eliminates figures entirely by 1944
- developed "drip painting" method (was called Jack the Dripper). He did not like the term "action painter"
- key element is line which is physically flung across the canvas on floor

VICTOR VASARELY (1908-1997)
- born in Hungry; moved to Paris to become an artist
- pioneer of Art of Optics — painting is kinetic
- believed that only through color can the full range of possibilities for optical painting be realized
- sets up retinal vibrations that dazzle the eye and bewilder perception

KENNETH NOLAND (born 1924)
- experimented with uniquely shaped canvases that became narrower and longer and became stripes
- some canvases were 30-foot long horizontal stripes
- bands separated by small stripes of raw canvas

Today we will use recycled (shredded) paper lines complete with texture (lettering from type) and possible added color…to create an abstract composition. Use colored markers in the strip sections first…NOT after they are glued!

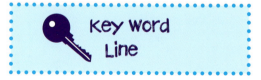
Key Word
Line

STEPS:
- color lines
- layout
- glue

ARTintegration

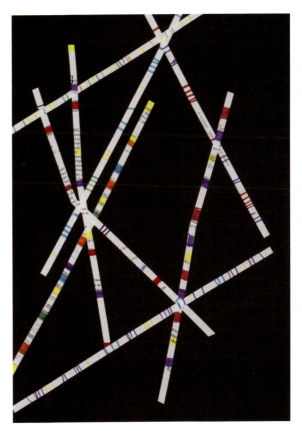

Student Work

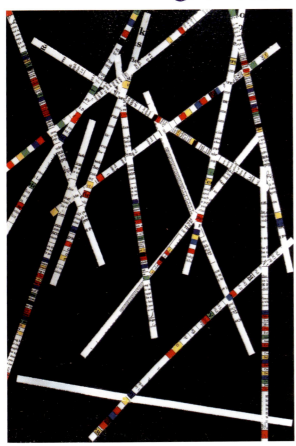
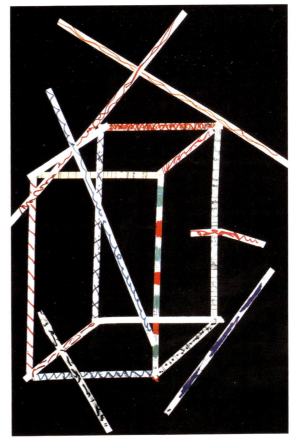

Wall Art
Social Studies/Science

> **criteria:**
> - Must draw one or two animals
> - Must create stone texture
> - Must use stick bones to paint

ELEMENTS OF ART:
Line, Shape, Color, Value, Form, Texture, and Space

MATERIALS:
12 x 18-inch light gray construction paper, pencil, paint, plastic plates (palette), beige and brown pastels, sticks (bones)

REFERENCE:
Animal artwork or photographs
Lascaux Cave art prints

VOCABULARY:
Incised, image, portrait, Lascaux, Cro-Magnons, Minoan, Pompeii, primitive, mammoth, fresco, migration, labyrinth, archeologist

ESSENTIAL QUESTIONS:
Why was wall art made?
Who were the Cro-Magnons?

NATIONAL STANDARDS: 1, 2, 3, 4, 5, 6

LEARNING OBJECTIVES:
Students will create animal art in the style of early cave artists using bones/sticks to paint.

INFORMATION:
LASCAUX CAVE (c. 15,000 BC)
- prehistoric men lived in caves and adorned the walls with art
- pictures in darkest recesses... reached by crawling on knees
- incised, painted, or sculpted images of horses, bison, and mammoth.
- prehistoric artists used scaffolding to create images high up on the walls
- sports huddle—they had primitive weapons and had to psych themselves up and use ceremony to instill courage for the hunt
- red, yellow and black from ground minerals. These were painted with moss, fingers, bones and horse hair, sticks

MINOAN ART (c. 2000 - 1500 BC)
- Crete (Mediterranean Island) was ruled by a powerful King Minos (My-nus) who built many cities with large palaces like Knossos
- 3,000 yrs. ago the civilization disappeared. Scholars think a volcano caused earthquakes and washed away the island.
- Archeologist, Sir Arthur Evan, uncovered 1200-room palace. It was a huge labyrinth. Walls decorated with frescoes. Pictures & statues of bulls considered sacred in their culture.

POMPEIAN ART (c. 200 BC - 79 AD)
- August 24, 79 AD, Mount Vesuvius (a volcano) erupted. Stones & ashes covered the Italian city of Pompeii in a few hours
- 200 yrs. later archeologists dug it out and discovered art and artifacts, one of which was a wall fresco of two people.

Today you will create an image that looks like a wall painting. Using sticks and bones, you will paint some animals of these ancient times.

> **Key Word**
> Cave Art

STEPS:
- sketch animals
- create cave walls background with chalk or pastels
- paint the animals using sticks and white/brown/black paint

ARTintegration

student work

Silhouette
Social Studies/Science

> **criteria:**
> - Must draw trunk/branches/twigs
> - Must paint flat
> - Measure to mount artwork

ELEMENTS OF ART:
Line, Shape, Color, Value, Form, Texture, and Space

MATERIALS:
White construction paper, pencil, scratch art paper, glue, black paint, detergent cups, paper towels, brushes, small plates

REFERENCE:
Hendrick Avercamp, *Winter Scene with Skaters Near a Castle*, Currier & Ives, *American Winter Sports*, Grandma Moses, *It Snows, Oh It Snows*

VOCABULARY:
Horizon line, silhouette, genre, lithography, primitive, shadow, tondo, overlap, background, foreground, Renaissance, profile, scene, profile

ESSENTIAL QUESTIONS:
What is a silhouette?
What is a profile?
What does primitive mean?
What does genre mean? What is perspective?

NATIONAL STANDARDS: 1, 2, 3, 4, 5, 6

LEARNING OBJECTIVES:
Students will paint a tree scene using a silhouette effect. Students will discuss ways of achieving perspective.

INFORMATION:
HENDRICK AVERCAMP (1585-1634))
- he specialized in skating scenes
- lived with his parents because he was speech and hearing impaired
- livens winter tones with red colors
- Tondo (circular painting from Renaissance)

CURRIER & IVES (1813-1895 and 1824-1895)
- explain process of lithography & mass production (show examples)
- have students discuss different ways of achieving perspective with trees: (1) size difference (2) atmospheric perspective (4) overlapping
- Lithography – printing method from 1859-1875 (replaced by newspaper)

GRANDMA MOSES (1860-1961)
- primitive artist who started painting when she was 76 years old and could no longer do needlepoint because of arthritis
- collected postcards to work from
- painted scenes from everyday life/cycles/seasons (genre scenes)

Today you will create a silhouette of a tree. Etienne Silhouette was a Frenchman who did small profile (cut-out) pictures of people. They are always one color, usually black. You will use black paint for your tree silhouettes. First sketch a horizon line with at least one large tree in the front. You can add more if you draw and paint quickly.

> **Key Word**
> Silhouette

STEPS:
- sketch tree on white paper
- draw final image on scratch art paper
- paint
- mount

ARTintegration

student work

Color Interaction
Art/Science

> **Criteria:**
> - Must use simple shape
> - Must place primaries together
> - Only two colors at a time together

ELEMENTS OF ART:
Line, Shape, Color, Value, Form, Texture, and Space

MATERIALS:
6 x 9-inch sheet of diffusing paper, pencil, markers, paper towels, spray bottles

REFERENCE:
Color by Ruth Heller
Examples of different artist's use of color

VOCABULARY:
Primary, secondary, tertiary, warm, cool, complementary, tint

ESSENTIAL QUESTIONS:
What are the primary colors?
What are the secondary colors?
What are warm colors? Cool colors?
Complementary colors?

NATIONAL STANDARDS: 1, 2, 5, 6

LEARNING OBJECTIVES:
Students will create a simple design by strategically placing colors near each other to create new colors when sprayed.

INFORMATION:
After reviewing the color wheel, ask who is an author? Who is an illustrator? Read book written and illustrated by Ruth Heller. Describe the colors between the primaries and the secondary colors. They are called tertiary colors. They are named with both primary and secondary colors..."yellow-orange" etc.

Today you may choose any simple shape to create a design while carefully placing colors next to each other ...both in the shapes you have chosen and around the shape leaving a little white space where the colors can bleed and blend. Example: circle of yellow with ring of orange around it.

Key words
Mixing color

STEPS:
- choose shape
- beginning with the primary colors, color each shape with one color, then color around the shape with another primary color. Continue coloring the shapes using secondary and tertiary colors, or complementary colors if desired.
- Markers do NOT touch!
- students may not use black or brown, but they can place complementary colors together to make brown/gray

ALTERNATE PROJECT (K-2):
Use only primary colors to study the interaction when they mix.

ARTintegration

student work

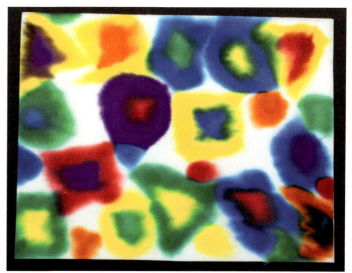

ARTintegration

NATIONAL STANDARDS FOR THE VISUAL ARTS

These standards provide a framework for helping students learn the characteristics of the visual arts by using a wide range of subject matter, symbols, meaningful images, and visual expressions, to reflect their ideas, feelings, and emotions; and to evaluate the merits of their efforts. The standards address these objectives in ways that promote acquisition of and fluency in new ways of thinking, working, communicating, reasoning, and investigating. They emphasize student acquisition of the most important and enduring ideas, concepts, issues, dilemmas, and knowledge offered by the visual arts. They develop new techniques, approaches, and habits for applying knowledge and skills in the visual arts to the world beyond school.

The visual arts are extremely rich. They range from drawing, painting, sculpture, and design, to architecture, film, video, and folk arts. They involve a wide variety of tools, techniques, and processes.

The standards are structured to recognize that many elements from this broad array can be used to accomplish specific educational objectives. For example, drawing can be used as the basis for creative activity, historical and cultural investigation, or analysis, as can any other fields within the visual arts. The standards present educational goals. It is the responsibility of practitioners to choose appropriately from this rich array of content and processes to fulfill these goals in specific circumstances and to develop the curriculum.

To meet the standards, students must learn vocabularies and concepts associated with various types of work in the visual arts and must exhibit their competence at various levels in visual, oral, and written form.

In Kindergarten–Grade 4, young children experiment enthusiastically with art materials and investigate the ideas presented to them through visual arts instruction. They exhibit a sense of joy and excitement as they make and share their artwork with others. Creation is at the heart of this instruction.

Students learn to work with various tools, processes, and media. They learn to coordinate their hands and minds in explorations of the visual world. They learn to make choices that enhance communicationof their ideas. Their natural inquisitiveness is promoted, and they learn the value of perseverance.

As they move from kindergarten through the early grades, students develop skills of observation, and they learn to examine the objects and events of their lives. At the same time, they grow in their ability to describe, interpret, evaluate, and respond to work in the visual arts. Through examination of their own work and that of other people, times, and places, students learn to unravel the essence of artwork and to appraise its purpose and value. Through these efforts, students begin to understand the meaning and impact of the visual world in which they live.

GRADES K-4

1. UNDERSTANDING AND APPLYING MEDIA, TECHNIQUES, AND PROCESSES
ACHIEVEMENT STANDARD:

- Students know the differences between materials, techniques, and processes
- Students describe how different materials, techniques, and processes cause different responses
- Students use different media, techniques, and processes to communicate ideas, experiences, and stories
- Students use art materials and tools in a safe and responsible manner

2. CONTENT STANDARD: USING KNOWLEDGE OF STRUCTURES AND FUNCTIONS
ACHIEVEMENT STANDARD:

- Students know the differences among visual characteristics and purposes of art in order to convey ideas
- Students describe how different expressive features and organizational principles cause different responses
- Students use visual structures and functions of art to communicate ideas

3. CHOOSING AND EVALUATING A RANGE OF SUBJECT MATTER, SYMBOLS, AND IDEAS
ACHIEVEMENT STANDARD:

- Students explore and understand prospective content for works of art
- Students select and use subject matter, symbols, and ideas to communicate meaning

4. UNDERSTANDING THE VISUAL ARTS IN RELATION TO HISTORY AND CULTURES
ACHIEVEMENT STANDARD:

- Students know that the visual arts have both a history and specific relationships to various cultures
- Students identify specific works of art as belonging to particular cultures, times, and places
- Students demonstrate how history, culture, and the visual arts can influence each other in making andstudying works of art

5. REFLECTING UPON AND ASSESSING THE CHARACTERISTICS AND MERITS OF THEIR WORK AND THE WORK OF OTHERS
ACHIEVEMENT STANDARD:

- Students understand there are various purposes for creating works of visual art
- Students describe how people's experiences influence the development of specific artworks
- Students understand there are different responses to specific artworks

6. MAKING CONNECTIONS BETWEEN VISUAL ARTS AND OTHER DISCIPLINES
ACHIEVEMENT STANDARD:

a. Students understand and use similarities and differences between characteristics of the visual arts and other arts disciplines
b. Students identify connections between the visual arts and other disciplines in the curriculum

GRADES 5-8

1. UNDERSTANDING AND APPLYING MEDIA, TECHNIQUES, AND PROCESSES
ACHIEVEMENT STANDARD:

- Students select media, techniques, and processes; analyze what makes them effective or not effective in communicating ideas; and reflect upon the effectiveness of their choices
- Students intentionally take advantage of the qualities and characteristics of art media, techniques, and processes to enhance communication of their experiences and ideas

2. USING KNOWLEDGE OF STRUCTURES AND FUNCTIONS
ACHIEVEMENT STANDARD:

- Students generalize about the effects of visual structures and functions and reflect upon these effects in their own work
- Students employ organizational structures and analyze what makes them effective or not effective in the communication of ideas
- Students select and use the qualities of structures and functions of art to improve communication of their ideas

3. CHOOSING AND EVALUATING A RANGE OF SUBJECT MATTER, SYMBOLS, AND IDEAS
ACHIEVEMENT STANDARD:

- Students integrate visual, spatial, and temporal concepts with content to communicate intended meaning in their artworks
- Students use subjects, themes, and symbols that demonstrate knowledge of contexts, values, and aesthetics that communicate intended meaning in artworks

4. UNDERSTANDING THE VISUAL ARTS IN RELATION TO HISTORY AND CULTURES
ACHIEVEMENT STANDARD:

- Students know and compare the characteristics of artworks in various eras and cultures
- Students describe and place a variety of art objects in historical and cultural contexts
- Students analyze, describe, and demonstrate how factors of time and place (such as climate, resources, ideas, and technology) influence visual characteristics that give meaning and value to a work of art

5. REFLECTING UPON AND ASSESSING THE CHARACTERISTICS AND MERITS OF THEIR WORK AND THE WORK OF OTHERS
ACHIEVEMENT STANDARD:

- Students compare multiple purposes for creating works of art
- Students analyze contemporary and historic meanings in specific artworks through cultural and aesthetic inquiry
- Students describe and compare a variety of individual responses to their own artworks and to artworks from various eras and cultures

6. MAKING CONNECTIONS BETWEEN VISUAL ARTS AND OTHER DISCIPLINES
ACHIEVEMENT STANDARD:

- Students compare the characteristics of works in two or more art forms that share similar subject matter, historical periods, or cultural context
- Students describe ways in which the principles and subject matter of other disciplines taught in the school are interrelated with the visual arts

GLOSSARY

ELEMENTS OF ART & PRINCIPLES OF DESIGN

line: the path of a point moving through space; it can vary in width, direction, curvature, length, and even color.

shape: an area contained within an implied line, or that is seen because of color or value changes. Shapes have two dimensions, length and width, and can be geometric or organic.

color: color depends on light because it is made of light. There must be light for us to see color. Hue, value, and intensity are the three main characteristics of color.

form: shape and form have the same qualities but shape is two-dimensional and form is three-dimensional; it describes volume and mass. Both may be freeform or geometric, natural or man-made.

space: actual space is a three-dimensional volume that has width, height, and depth. Space in a painting is an illusion that creates a feeling of depth. Paintings are divided into positive space (the object itself) and negative space (the surrounding area).

texture: refers to the surface quality, both simulated and actual, of artwork. Using a dry brush technique creates simulated texture while heavy application of paint produces actual texture.

value: value refers to dark and light; the value scale refers to black and white with all gradations of gray in between. Value contrasts help us to understand a two-dimensional work of art.

balance: balance refers to the distribution of visual weight in a work of art. Balance can be either symmetrical or asymmetrical.

contrast: differences in values, colors, textures, shapes, and other elements. Contrast creates visual excitement and adds interest to the work. If all the elements ~ value, for example ~ are the same, the result is monotonous and unexciting.

emphasis: emphasis creates dominance and focus. Artists can emphasize color, value, shapes, or other art elements to achieve dominance. Contrast can be used to emphasize a center of interest.

movement: movement directs viewers through a work, often to a focal area. Movement can be directed along lines, edges, shapes, and colors, but moves the eye most easily on paths of equal value.

pattern: pattern uses elements in planned or random repetitions in a work of art. Pattern increases visual excitement by enriching surface interest.

rhythm: rhythm is the repetition of visual movement ~ colors, shapes, or lines. Movement and rhythm work together to create the visual equivalent of a musical beat.

unity: visual unity is one of the most important aspects of well-designed art. Unity provides the cohesive quality that makes a work feel complete.

VOCABULARY

abdomen: the posterior part of the body of an arthropod, especially the segments of an insect's body behind the thorax.

abstract: art which utilizes simplified or symbolic forms; subject matter may be recognizable or may be completely transformed into shapes, colors, and/or lines.

adjacent: next to or adjoining something else

Africa: the second largest continent; located to the south of Europe and bordered to the west by the South Atlantic and to the east by the Indian Ocean.

antennae: a pair of long, thin sensory appendages on the heads of insects, crustaceans, and some other arthropods.

applique: a decorative design made of one material sewn over another.

apprentice: a person who is learning a trade from a skilled employer.

angle: the space (usually measured in degrees) between two intersecting lines or surfaces at the point where they meet.

arc: a curved shape, or something shaped like a curve.

arch: a curved symmetrical structure spanning an opening and supporting the weight of a bridge, roof, or wall above it.

archeologist: a scientist who studies prehistoric people and their culture.

architecture: the art and science of designing buildings or other structures.

author: a writer of a book, article, or report.

background: the part of an image that serves as a setting to the main figures or objects, or that appears furthest from the viewer.

Bavaria: a Germanic state whose history, first as a duchy and later as a kingdom and republic, dates from the sixth century.

bishop: a senior member of the Christian clergy.

blend: merge colors together so that one is not clearly distinguishable from the other.

block: a piece of wood or metal engraved for printing on paper or fabric

calligraphy: The art of producing decorative handwriting or lettering with a pen or brush.

camouflage: the disguising of military personnel, equipment, and installations by painting or covering them to make them blend in with their surroundings.

cartouche: an oval enclosing a group of Egyptian hieroglyphs, typically representing the name and title of a monarch.

cathedral: a large and important church.

celebration: a joyful occasion for special festivities to mark some happy event.

cell: the smallest structural and functional unit of an organism.

Chinese: a native or national of China, or a person of Chinese descent.

civilization: the society, culture, and way of life of a particular area.

colonial: relating to the period of the British colonies in America before independence.

coloring: textile design in the same pattern showing different color combinations.

compass: an instrument for drawing circles and arcs.

ART integration

complementary colors: colors that are opposite one another on the color wheel. When placed side by side, these colors offer the maximum contrast produce optical vibrations. When mixed together they become subdued and produce grayed variations of the original colors.

composition: the arrangement and organization of the elements of design into a relationship planned by the artist.

compound eye: an eye consisting of many small visual units, as found in insects.

contemporary: belonging to the present time.

contour: the edge or line which depicts an edge. In a drawing, a contour line is used to show the shape of an object in space or the surfaces of objects or figures.

cool colors: hues in the violet to green range of the spectrum or color wheel.

costume: a set of clothes in a style typical of a particular country or historical period.

creature: a fictional or imaginary being, typically a frightening one

Cro-Magnon: the first early modern humans; from approx 35,000 years ago.

cross-hatching: a method of showing value by using parallel lines at different angles that get darker as they are drawn closer together.

cube: symmetrical three-dimensional shape, either solid or hollow, contained by six equal squares.

culture: The customs, arts, social institutions, and achievements of a particular nation, people, or other social group

curve: a line or outline that gradually deviates from being straight for some or all of its length.

decorative: serving to make something look more attractive; ornamental.

design: plan or organization of parts to form a coordinated whole.

diagonal: a slanting straight pattern or line.

diamond: a figure with four straight sides of equal length forming two opposite acute angles and two opposite obtuse angles.

dowry: property or money brought by a bride to her husband on their marriage.

dragon: a mythical monster like a giant reptile. In European tradition the dragon is typically fire-breathing and tends to symbolize chaos or evil, whereas in the Far East it is usually a beneficent symbol associated with water and the heavens

dynasty: a line of hereditary rulers of a country.

eggs: an approximately spherical or ellipsoidal body produced by birds, snakes, insects and other animals housing the embryo during its development.

Egyptian: a native of ancient or modern Egypt, or a person of Egyptian descent.

embroidery: the art of decorating fabric or other materials with needle and thread.

emigrant: a person who leaves their own country to settle permanently in another.

emperor: a supreme ruler of great power and rank, especially one ruling an empire.

exoskeleton: a hard, jointed, external covering that encloses the muscles and organs of an organism; typical of many arthropods including insects.

festival: an event in a local community, which centers on and celebrates some unique aspect of that community.

floral: decorated with or depicting flowers

fluorescent: brilliantly colored and apparently giving off light.

foreground: the part of a view that is closest to the observer in a painting or photograph.

found object: common or unusual objects that may be used to create a work of art; specifically refers to scrap, discarded materials that have been "found."

fraktur: elaborate illuminated folk art created by the Pennsylvania Dutch

fresco: a mural done with watercolors on wet plaster.

functional: designed to be practical and useful, rather than solely to be attractive.

gargoyle: a carved face or figure projecting from the gutter of a building, typically acting as a spout to carry water clear of a wall.

genre: a category of artistic composition, as in music or literature, characterized by similarities in form, style, or subject matter.

geometric shapes: regular shapes most often found in human-made objects and architecture, including circles, ovals, squares, rectangles, and triangles.

glass: a hard, brittle substance, typically transparent or translucent, made by fusing sand with soda, lime, and sometimes other ingredients and cooling rapidly.

glaze: in ceramics, a thin coating that is fused to a clay object by firing in a kiln.

Gothic: style of art in Europe (during the 12th through 15th centuries) which emphasized religious art and architecture with strong vertical lines, spires, and pointed arches.

guild: an association of craftsmen or merchants, often having considerable power.

happening: a performance, event, or situation meant to be considered art, usually as performance art.

hard-edge: painting in which abrupt transitions are found between color areas.

hex signs: a form of Pennsylvania Dutch folk art, related to fraktur, found in the Fancy Dutch tradition in Pennsylvania Dutch Country

hexagon: a plane figure with six straight sides and six angles.

hieroglyphics: a writing system using picture symbols; used in ancient Egypt.

highlight: a bright or reflective area in a painting, picture, or design.

holiday: a day on which work is suspended by law or custom.

horizon line: implied line formed as an apparent boundary between earth and sky.

horizontal: parallel to the plane of the horizon; at right angles to the vertical.

illusion: a thing that is or is likely to be wrongly perceived or interpreted by the senses.

illustrator: a person who creates pictures for magazines, books, advertising, etc.

imagination: the ability of the mind to be creative or resourceful.

incise: to mark an object or surface with a cut or a series of cuts.

insect: a small arthropod animal that has six legs and generally one or two pairs of wings.

ARTintegration

intersect: divide something by passing or lying across it.

kachina: a god-like ancestral spirit in the mythology of Pueblo Indians.

kinetic art: three-dimensional art that contains moving parts or changing visual patterns.

labyrinth: a complicated irregular network of passages or paths in which it is difficult to find one's way; a maze.

larvae: the immature form of an insect.

Lascaux: the site of a cave in the Dordogne, France, containing Paleolithic wall paintings.

lead: a soft heavy metal that holds stained glass in place

legend: a traditional story popularly regarded as historical but unauthenticated.

lithography: printmaking process in which a design is created on a flat, specially prepared stone or metal plate, and ink impressions from this are made when placed against paper and run through a press.

loom: frame or device in which fibers are woven into fabric by the crossing of threads (called weft) over and under stationary threads (called warp).

mammoth: a large extinct elephant of the Pleistocene epoch, typically hairy with a sloping back and long curved tusks.

metamorphosis: the process in an insect of transformation from an immature form to an adult form in two or more distinct stages.

migration: movement of people to a new area or country in order to find work or better living conditions

Minoan: of, relating to, or denoting a Bronze Age civilization centered on Crete (c.3000–1050 BC), its people, or its language.

monument: a statue, building, or other structure erected to commemorate a famous or notable person or event.

motif: the underlying idea, the dominant theme, or the distinctive element of design found in a work of art.

myth: a traditional story, especially one concerning the early history of a people or explaining some natural phenomenon, and typically involving supernatural beings

negative space: area around objects sometimes called the background in a two-dimensional work of art.

nonobjective: art that has no recognizable subject matter; emphasis is on the color or composition of the work itself.

optical: of or relating to sight, especially in relation to the action of light.

organ: a part of an organism that is typically self-contained and has a specific vital function, such as the heart or liver in humans

organic shapes: shapes that are free flowing, informal and irregular such as leaves, seashells, and flowers.

orphan: a child who has lost both parents.

outline: a line enclosing or indicating the shape of an object in an artwork.

overlap: extend over so as to cover partly.

paisley: a distinctive intricate pattern of curved, feather-shaped figures based on a pine-cone design from India.

palette: a thin board or slab on which an artist lays and mixes colors.

papyrus: a thick paper-like material produced from the papyrus plant of Egypt.

parallel: lines, planes, surfaces, or objects that are side by side and have the same distance continuously between them

parallelogram: a four-sided plane rectilinear figure with opposite sides parallel.

patchwork: needlework in which small pieces of cloth in different designs, colors, or textures are sewn together.

Pennsylvania Dutch: immigrants and their descendants from southwestern Germany and Switzerland who settled in Pennsylvania in the 17th and 18th centuries.

perpendicular: at an angle of 90° to a given line, plane, or surface.

plaid: any fabric woven of differently colored yarns in a crossbarred pattern.

poem: a piece of writing that partakes of the nature of both speech and song, and that is usually rhythmical and metaphorical.

pointillism: a technique of neo-Impressionist painting using tiny dots, which become blended in the viewer's eye.

Pompeii: an ancient city in Italy buried by an eruption of Mount Vesuvius in AD 79.

portrait: a drawing, painting, or print of a person.

positive space: objects or parts of a work of art (as opposed to the "negative" background or space around the objects).

primary colors: the three main colors (red, yellow, and blue) that can be combined to make all other colors.

primitive: relating to, denoting, or preserving an early stage in the evolutionary or historical development of something.

print: an original work of art made from one of the printmaking processes.

printmaking: the art of making prints using relief printmaking, intaglio, lithography, or serigraphy.

profile: an outline of something, esp. a person's face, as seen from one side.

proportion: comparative size relationship between several objects or between parts of objects in a work of art.

protractor: an instrument for measuring angles, typically in the form of a flat semicircle marked with degrees along the curved edge.

Pueblo tale: traditional story, legen, or myth of ancient communities of Native Americans in the southwestern United States

pupal: an inactive stage of insect development (when it is not feeding) intermediate between larva and adult

pyramid: a monumental structure with a square or triangular base and sloping sides that meet in a point at the top, esp. one built of stone as a royal tomb in ancient Egypt

quilt: bed covering made of padding enclosed between layers of fabric and kept in place by lines of stitching, typically applied in a decorative design

rectangle: a plane figure with four straight sides and four right angles, especially one with unequal adjacent sides.

rectangular solid: a three-dimensional object with six sides which are all rectangles.

recycle: to process used or abandoned materials for use in creating new products.

relief surface: surface which projects from a background of which it is a part; refers to sculpture or to a type of printmaking in which raised surfaces are inked.

relief sculpture: sculpture in which a design or image is carved into a flat surface.

Renaissance: a period of time (about 1400 through 1600) in Europe characterized by cultural awareness, interest, and learning

resist: substance applied to plate to protect it from acid while etching metal plate. Also called a "ground."

Romanesque: the art and architecture of Western Europe from approximately AD 1000 to the 13th century or later

rosetta stone: a large inscribed stone found near Rosetta, Egypt, in 1799; used as a basis for understanding many examples of hieroglyphic writing.

sacred: devoted or dedicated to a deity or to some religious purpose.

scene: the place where an incident in real life or fiction occurs or occurred.

sculpture: three-dimensional pieces of art that have been molded, cast, carved, or constructed.

secondary colors: colors that contain equal amounts of the two primary colors adjacent to them on the color wheel. Orange, green, and violet are the secondary colors.

secular: having no religious or spiritual basis

settler: a person who has migrated to an area and established permanent residence there, often to colonize the area.

sgraffito: decoration by cutting away parts of a surface layer (as of plaster or clay) to expose a different colored ground.

shade: darkening of a hue made by adding black to a color.

shading: graduated variations in value often used to give a feeling of volume, form, and depth.

shadow: a dark area or shape produced by a body coming between light and a surface.

silhouette: the dark shape and outline of someone or something visible against a lighter background.

silk: thread or fabric made from the fiber produced by the silkworm

solstice: either of the two times of the year when the sun is at its greatest distance from the equator

sphere: a round solid figure, or its surface, with every point on its surface equidistant from its center.

square: a plane figure with four equal straight sides and four right angles.

still life: a painting or drawing that uses inanimate objects as subject matter.

stipple: the creation of a pattern simulating varying degrees of solidity or shading by using small dots.

symbol: a thing that represents or stands for something else, esp. a material object representing something abstract.

symmetrical: exact reflection of form on opposite sides of a dividing line or plane.

system: a set of organs in the body with a common structure or function.

tertiary: colors created by mixing primary and secondary colors – red-orange, yellow-orange, yellow-green, blue-green, blue-violet, and red-violet.

textile: a type of cloth or woven fabric.

theory: a supposition or a system of ideas intended to explain something, esp. one based on general principles independent of the thing to be explained.

thorax: the part of an insect's body that lies between the head and the abdomen.

three-dimensional: having height, length, and width, as, for example, a sculpture.

tint: lightening of a hue made by adding a color to white.

tissue: any of the distinct types of material of which animals or plants are made, consisting of specialized cells and their products.

tomb: a large vault, typically an underground one, for burying the dead

tondo: a Renaissance term for a circular work of art, either a painting or a sculpture.

trace: to copy a drawing or design by drawing over its lines on a superimposed piece of transparent paper

transfer: to copy a drawing or design from one surface to another

translucent: allowing light, but not detailed images, to pass through; semitransparent.

transparent: object or material through which light can pass. Stained glass windows and watercolor paintings are examples of objects in which transparent media have been used.

triangle: a plane figure with three straight sides and three angles.

vertical: at right angles to a horizontal plane; having an alignment such that the top is directly above the bottom.

vibration: effect that occurs when complementary colors are placed side by side in a work of art.

visualize: to form a mental picture of something that is invisible or abstract

warm colors: hues in the red to yellow range of the spectrum or color wheel.

warp: the threads which are extended lengthwise in a loom or frame and which are crossed by the weft threads.

weaving: a textile in which two distinct sets of yarns or threads, called the warp and the weft are interlaced to form a fabric or cloth.

weft: the threads used to create color, texture, pattern, and design in a weaving; often carried across the warp threads during the weaving process.

wizard: a person who has magical powers, especially in legends and fairy tales.

worship: to treat someone or something with the reverence appropriate to a deity

woven: formed by interlacing long threads passing in one direction with others at a right angle to them.

ABOUT THE AUTHOR

I grew up on Long Island, New York, steeped in the arts. Although we only went into NYC a few times during the year for musicals and Radio City, the public school systems were great. While a special aunt of mine paid for my siblings and me to take piano lessons (along with art lessons, ballet, tap and jazz, swimming, diving, etc.), I was handed a cello in 4th grade with free private weekly lessons through 12th grade! The same was true for my brother and sister with their instruments of choice. By 7th grade, an oboe was added with free lessons during lunch time because I could only miss one class a week for a music lesson. In art, everyone took excellent basic art classes for 7th and 8th grade…and thereafter it was by choice.

Going to Smith College was another incredible educational experience. Starting out as a math major changed after the 2nd semester of Calculus! I majored in art knowing that I wanted to teach, continued with piano lessons, and sang with the Smith College choir. The choir traveled all over Europe singing in Cathedrals and visiting castles. I was the photographer for the group and enjoyed everything about the experiences and traveling.

Next was graduate school at Pratt Institute for a Master of Fine Arts. While working on that degree, however, I discovered textile design. After graduating, I turned down a teaching job for what I thought would be just a moment to work in New York City in textiles. I ended up at Fieldcrest Mills and worked there as a designer/stylist for just under four years. After relocating to Greensboro, North Carolina, I taught at the Greensboro Art Center and developed my own textile design business. It was some 15 years later before I went into the public school system to teach art. I taught over 600 3-5th graders for over ten years. Then our school became a year-round magnet school where I now teach art and music to grades K-5.

When I arrived at New Vision School, there were textbooks for 3-5th grades that were already 15 years old. New textbooks were not an option. Because my two sons were in elementary school at this point, it was easy for me to create art lesson plans that integrated with their core classes. In addition, there were always lessons created by request from grade level teachers. These were then placed into an order using art curriculum and developing art skills similar to my student teaching experience at the Smith College Day School. There we had developed units focusing on and exploring one element of art (line). Kicking it up a notch 20 years later, every class was started by listing the elements of art and how they would be used in the day's art lesson. Because the youngest were 3rd graders and had arrived believing only some were artists, I started the yearly program lessons with the dot (texture)…becoming a line, then an outline, a shape, and then a 3-D form. The goal was to prove to them as they progressed through the art projects that they could have success and all were indeed "artists." The format and progression of art skills then remained the same each year with new lesson plans developed to fit into the element of art in the sequence.